The Good Ole' Days
Autobiography of a Farm Boy

Written by Milton J. Hayman

Edited by
Marilyn Hayman, Jo Anne Agrimson,
Joe Deden and Mary Bell,
Tom Hayman and Martha Turner

Book Layout and Design by
Sarah Peterson, Peterson Creative Photography & Design

Layout Design and Production created in Adobe InDesign

Published by No Place Publishing

All Rights Reserved © 2024

No part of this publication may be reproduced, distributed, or transmitted in any form or by any means, including photocopying, recording, or other electronic or mechanical methods, without the prior written permission of the publisher, except as permitted by U.S. copyright law. For permission requests, contact No Place Publishing, Attn: TJ Hayman, 40W704 Timbergate Lane, St. Charles, IL 60175.

First Edition

ISBN# 979-8-218-52407-4

Distributed by IngramSpark

"The Good Ole' Days"
AUTOBIOGRAPHY OF A FARM BOY

This book is dedicated to my father Milton Hayman, the author. My father was a sensitive and thoughtful person with an adventuresome spirit and a playful sense of humor. I am sure much of his personality evolved from his love of reading the great works and immersing himself in opera, classical music and nature. He loved traveling internationally and learning about the people, history, arts and geography. He possessed a wonderful sense of humor and was endlessly playful. He was introspective about life and had the philosophy of Carpe Diem.

He wrote the following history of growing up in the late 1920s, 1930s and 1940s to give our family a unique perspective of life in rural Minnesota. He organized his thoughts of the early years by describing what activities occurred in each month of the year—a real eye opener for us today. He referred to it as the "Good Ole' Days" but now that will be judged by the reader.

My mother Marilyn Hayman encouraged him to write down his stories. One can clearly pick up his sense of humor through his writing and describing the activities. We are pleased to share his writings with you.

Dad, thank you for documenting these memories. I will forever miss you, think about you and love you.

Tom Hayman

"Nothing you love is lost. Not really. Things, people—they always go away, sooner or later. You can't hold them, any more than you can hold moonlight. But if they've touched you, if they're inside you, then they're still yours. The only things you ever really have are the ones you hold inside your heart."

-Bruce Coville

Acknowledgments

This book is about family, about what it was like growing up during the Depression on a rural farm in southern Minnesota. It was assembled by Milt and Marilyn with input from Milt's siblings and their son Tom Hayman and daughter-in-law Martha Turner. The voice is all Milty. Our thanks to Robert Hayman, Wilbur Hayman, Adeline Hayman Deden and Janet Hayman Golisch for their insights and inputs. Marilyn edited the original text. Tom and Martha provided text, photos and financing to publish this book.

Nieces and nephews reviewed the documents and submitted materials and photographs. Our thanks to Bill and Jon Hayman; Dan and Jean Hayman; Niles, Joe and Ross Deden; Lisa Trueblood; Sara Heintz; Tim Golisch and Ben Golisch. A special thank you to Jean Hayman, the keeper of early family photos and for making them available in a digital format.

Joe Deden and Mary Bell took Milt and Marilyn's original document and worked with a design team that included Jo Anne Agrimson (copy editor) and Sarah Peterson (Peterson Creative Photography & Design) to shape the design and layout. They were a great creative team!

Kathy Sundstedt did a deep read and made wonderful suggestions.

Charles Hayman was an early photographer and this book is enhanced by his photos.

A special thanks to Goodhue County Historical Society, Fillmore County Historical Society, Minnesota Historical Society and St. Louis County Historical Society for the use of photos.

We hope that the family members and others reading this book will appreciate learning about rural life in the 1930s and 1940s as much as Milton enjoyed recounting the history.

Family photo circa 1932/33. Edith, Wilbur, Dora, Robert, Adeline and Milt. Janet was born in 1939.

Contents

Acknowledgements	i
Family Portrait	iii
"A Theme of Life's Indefiniteness"	iv
Farm Map	v
Introduction	vi
The Hayman Family 1821-2016	vii
Autobiography Of A Farm Boy	1
Head Cheese	1
Firewood, It Heats You Many Times	5
Winter Chores	9
Springtime	11
A Full Potato Bin	14
Tree Forts and Caves	15
Make Hay While the Sun Shines	18
Threshing Crew	21
Dog Days of Summer	27
Stone Foundations	29
Gofer Jobs	31
Bozo, the Wonder Dog	32
Harvest Moon	33
The Universal Tinkerer	36
Get-Togethers	39
Inventive Ways to Have Fun	45
Floods	48
The Woeful Ones	49
Mutt's Glory	51
Lilacs	53
Fourth of July	55
A Swarm of Bees	57
Willow Bush Farm	59
Early School Years: District 90	61
Nimrod, God of the Hunt	69
Hired Men	71
Yellowstone	73
Vignettes	75
High School and College Years	81
Maiden Rock Neighbors	89
Epilogue	93
So what happened to the people in this book?	94
Glossary	96

That's me, front row, bottom left—the happy, smiling one with the mischievous look on my face.

The Haymans, 1940. Back row: Edith (18), Wilbur (20), Adeline (16)
Front row: Milt (12) Dora (42), Janet (2), Charles (47), Bob (22)

"A theme of life's indefiniteness"
- Evans

Adeline and Milt enjoying a mud puddle. Adeline, 4 years older than Milt, was his closest playmate.

Please forgive me if I have stolen a phrase or two from far greater writers without giving credit. Caldwell, in *God's Little Acre* lifted "…her rising beauties" from Cervantes, as did Fielding, in describing *Tom Jones*, "…for every Man is as Heaven made him, and sometimes a great deal worse." D. H. Lawrence lifted "John Thomas" from Rabelais and used it in *Lady Chatterly's Lover*. That said, we'll all be equal in the box.

For Tom and Martha—and later in life for Andrew and Michael—if there is one of the thousands of tidbits of philosophy I would like you to remember, it is this one:

> "He has spent his life best, who has enjoyed it most."
> Samuel Butler

The concept of pleasure and happiness prevails in every "Great" work of literature. Cervantes, again:

> "The Happy have whole days, and those they choose; the Unhappy have but hours, and those they lose."

The following history is as I remember it—through my eyes. As you read this narrative, ponder this line from Butler's *The Way of all Flesh*.

> "My boy, you must not judge by the work, but by the work in connection with the surroundings."

The Depression!

> "It was the best of times; it was the worst of times."
> Charles Dickens

The Hayman "Willow Bush" Farm
Red Wing, Minnesota

Original address simply: Route 3, Red Wing, MN
Current address: 31891 Cty 45 Blvd, Red Wing, MN 55066
GPS: 42" 29' 10" N, 92" 29' 06" W

Introduction

My wife Marilyn talked me into writing this book. One of my reasons for doing so was this was a time, that ever was or ever will be, of the greatest changes in farming history. We went from oxen and horses—used for thousands of years—to jet travel and placing a man on the moon. All in one generation!

It was a time before automobiles and farm tractors; before electricity and cell phones; before running water and indoor plumbing; before central heat or air conditioning.

Young people today wouldn't dream of standing in a fresh cow pie to warm cold bare feet or going to school in a room with no lights other than the windows. Some people call those the good ole' days. If they call those days *good*, they have forgotten the hardship. If they call those days *good* they remember the tight family bonds that living and working close together forged.

I miss the more natural pace of life that the changing seasons of the era demanded. We have more "labor-saving" devices today but they certainly don't make the day any longer to accomplish all the things our hectic lifestyle demands.

The great changes that affected both farming and transportation came from electricity and the mobile combustion engine. This unique period of farming history could be lost to our family if not recorded. I felt it is important for our son, his family and our family as a whole, to have a perspective from which to appreciate their lives and our heritage.

When you read these stories, certainly think of the hard work that was required, but also think of the pride and sense of accomplishment we felt in having both a full pantry and potato bin at the end of the growing season and a neatly mowed hay field or a corn field planted so accurately it could be cultivated in two directions.

I would like to thank my life-long love and happiness, Marilyn, for all her work in getting this book published. Without her dedicated help, this history would never have been completed.

Brothers Bob and Willy's input about our early history also deserves special note.

(Editor's Note: Now, years later, we must also thank Milt's nephew, Joe Deden and his wife Mary Bell for helping to expedite the publication of this work.)

Milton Hayman circa 1946 Senior Red Wing High School photo.

The Hayman Family
1821-2016

1821 — Wm. Hayman Sr. born
London, England

William Hayman Sr. was a Chartist in England. He believed all men should have the right to vote and sought to improve the conditions of working men. This workers' rights movement reached its peak in 1848, when William became discouraged and moved to the US. His family lived in a sod hut for the first five years before building a home in 1860.

The Hungry 1840s
In the early 1840s Britain experienced an economic depression accompanied by several years of bad harvests. The 1845 potato blight appeared in England and Scotland and spread, causing the great Irish famine of 1846.

The Hungry 40s

1843 — Wm. Hayman Jr. born

1849 — Wm. Hayman Sr. *Leaves England with his wife, Wm. Jr. and daughter Sophie*

1855 — Wm. Hayman Sr. *Leaves PA and homesteads in MN*

— 1858 Minnesota Statehood

1861–1865 Civil War

— 1870 Maria "Gim" Peters born

Wm. Hayman Jr. marries Maria "Gim" Peters — 1891 Sarah Hayman dies of typhoid and Wm. Jr. goes blind from it
— 1893 Charles William Hayman born

— 1901 Wm. Hayman Sr. dies (age 80)

William Hayman Sr. was born in 1821 in London, England. He emigrated to the US in 1849 and settled in Pennsylvania and then left there in 1855 and homesteaded in Minnesota.

Left to right: Wm. Hayman Jr., Sarah Moser (Wm. Hayman Jr.'s first wife), Mr. Moser, Mrs. Wm. Hayman Sr., Wm. Hayman Sr., Sophie Hayman Benson (Wm. Hayman Jr.'s sister).

Timeline

1914–1918 WWI

1917 — Milt's Parents Charles Hayman and Dorothea Issendorf marry

- 1918 (brother) Robert "Bob" Hayman born
- 1920 (brother) Wilbur "Willy" Hayman born
- 1922 (sister) Edith Hayman born
- 1924 (sister) Adeline Hayman born

1928 — Milton Hayman (Milt) born

- 1928 Wm. Hayman Jr. dies (age 85)

1929–1939 Great Depression

1939–1945 WWII

- 1939 (sister) Janet Hayman born
- 1941 United States enters WWII
- 1944 (sister) Edith Hayman dies (age 21)
- 1946 Milt graduates high school and enters military service (1946-48)
- 1947 Milt's parents, Charles and Dora build a new home (brother) Wilbur and wife Fran move into the farm home

1952 — Milton Hayman marries Marilyn Fiedler

- 1953 (son) Thomas "Tom" Hayman born
- 1956 Maria "Gim" (Peters) Hayman dies (age 86)

Dora and Charles were married 60 years when Charles died in 1977. They lived their lives in Red Wing, Minnesota and reared six children.

1968 — Milton and Marilyn moved to Prior Lake, MN

1975 — Milton and Marilyn moved to Maiden Rock, WI

- 1977 (father) Charles Hayman dies (age 84)
- 1978 (mother) Dora Hayman dies (age 80)

Marilyn and Milton's marriage lasted for 60 years until 2016 when Milton died. Marilyn currently lives in St Charles, Illinois, near their son Tom, his wife Martha and his sons Andrew and Michael.

- 1990 (grandson) Andrew Hayman born
- 1992 (grandson) Michael Hayman born
- 1999 (sister) Janet Hayman Golisch dies (age 59)
- 2003 (brother) Robert Hayman dies (age 85)
- 2007 (brother) Wilbur "Willy" Hayman dies (age 87)

2012 — Milton Hayman dies (age 84)

- 2016 (sister) Adeline Hayman Deden dies (age 93)

Head Cheese

Our annual work cycle began right after the New Year with butchering three hogs and, later, one beef. The hogs, shot with Dad's 22 Special, were gutted and pulled up in a tree with rope and pulley. They were lowered into a 50-gallon wooden barrel of scalding hot water that had been heated in an iron kettle over a wood fire in the "cook shanty." The shanty was a small building made of cottonwood boards. Water in this building came from a dry well, where a long rod was used to turn the water on and off to prevent freezing.

After scalding, the hog was pulled from the water and swung onto a door laid on saw horses. It was then scraped with a sharp-edged metal disc with a wood handle called a hog scraper. When all the hair was removed, the hog rind, or skin, was smooth, clean and white. Using a pulley, two or three men would hoist each hog up by hand into a tree. This kept them out of reach of our dogs. The carcasses were washed down with boiling water and then left to dry. Each year our neighbor, Charlie Sip, would rub his hand over the carcass and pat it and say, "Smooth as a school teacher's ass."

At the end of the day, they were cut in half with a meat saw or axe, hauled to the back kitchen and hooked onto the rafters with an iron "S" looped into the leg and left for further processing in the days to come.

Grindstones were used to sharpen kitchen cutlery, hoes and axes.

Charlie Sip helped, in return for the pig livers, which our family did not care for. Charlie usually got a shot of brandy before going home. He was the father of Donnie and Robbie, neighborhood friends I grew up with.

Charlie was a stonemason of fair repute. Goodhue County hired him to lay the end walls and the four wings, which extended out along the banks of many small country bridges. It took a good man to handle those large limestone blocks. Later, when poured concrete came into use, he was left without a trade. The first county-engineered bridges over Wells Creek were of poured concrete and they all washed out in a big flood. None of Charlie's stone bridges ever washed out and some are still standing around the county. Sadly, the one by the site of our District 90 School was still in perfect shape when it was demolished in 1998.

After a week or two of gorging on fresh, sweet pork, we'd butcher a beef. It was skinned and quartered. The intestines were saved and cleaned in the snow, then rinsed thoroughly with water, to be used as sausage casing for liver sausage and blood sausage, with little squares of white fat in it. Both were quite salty and delicious served on soda crackers. Summer sausage was made with lots of pepper and yellow peppercorns. Well-preserved, it lasted long into the summer.

The intestines were filled using a cylinder-shaped sausage machine, 10" in diameter, with a capacity of about 2 gallons of prepared sausage mixture. A heavy, flat circular plate placed on top of the meat had a system of gears with a hand crank that pressed down on the plate, forcing the meat down. At the bottom of the cylinder was an opening with a metal "spout" where the casing was attached. As pressure was exerted on the plate, the sausage mixture was forced out of the cylinder, through the spout and into the sausage casing which had been cut to the desired length and knotted on the opposite end. The casing material was flexible and would stretch allowing for sausages of different sizes. Some were made into small 8" to 10" circles to cook on the stove and others were fatter and cut 12 to 16 inches in length.

All sausages were hung in the smokehouse and suspended from three-foot long wooden bars and then smoked for a week with smoldering corn cobs, producing the required smoke. The smokehouse was a beautiful sight to see and smell, this 7' x 10' building filled with sausage, hams, bacon and large chunks of beef to dry-smoke.

Curing meats was a long and involved process. Hams, bacon and beef were rubbed with salt and needed to stand for several days. Then they were taken into the basement, packed into separate 20-30-gallon stoneware crocks and covered with salt brine. Saltpeter was added to give the meat a reddish color. Brown sugar was added to the bacon. A heavy plate was placed on top of each crock to keep the meat covered with brine.

How to make Grit-Wurst (Head Cheese)

This German dish is mainly made from a pig's head. The Haymans used an English version. I imagine that is how Grandpa changed his German wife's recipe. Most German recipes just cook the head, add raisins to it and it tastes very porky.

After cooking the pig's head, the Haymans saved the broth, which they poured over steel cut oats and added a lot of ground up onions, salt and pepper, a teaspoon or two of cloves, and a tablespoon of allspice. It was mixed up and baked in the oven until the fat became clear. Then it was cut into smaller pieces, wrapped and frozen. Wilbur said when times were tough on the farm, they'd even grind up the pig's ears and use them in the mix too!

Preserving the tradition of making grit sausage in 2007 are Sister Adeline Deden and nephews Bill Hayman, Ross Deden and Joe Deden.

Mother checked the brine regularly. If it began to smell sour, the meat would be taken out and washed. The brine would be boiled, more salt added and the meat and brine returned to the crocks. This process usually took four to six weeks.

The hog fat was ground and then cooked on the wood stove to make lard. This took several days. Some of the lard was saved in small stone crocks for cooking, especially to fry potatoes. There was no finer flaky pie crust than that made using fresh lard. The rest was used to make laundry soap, and that was another 2- to 3-day job. The lard was boiled with lye and other ingredients and then poured into 16" x 24" soap boxes 3" deep. It was left to set and cool until somewhat firm, then cut into 2.5" x 3" x 3" bars. It couldn't set too long, or it would harden and be difficult to cut into smaller bars.

Butchering a hog. Little was wasted: even the intestines were used as sausage casings. Wilbur said during the hard years, even the ears were ground and made into head cheese. Goodhue County Historical Society Photo.

The next related chore was to make grit-wurst from the meat of the hogs' heads, which were no small job to clean. After it was cooked, Dad had the job of carefully removing all the meat, which was ground up with huge quantities of pepper, salt and onions. This was all mixed and cooked with steel cut oats, then placed into small stone crocks to be eaten for breakfast all winter, spring and early summer. Sometimes it was sliced and baked in the oven until brown and was served with honey and buckwheat pancakes. The pancakes were made using a yeast starter. Mom always left a little for the next morning. Occasionally, we had bacon for a change.

Beef was also preserved. My personal favorite was the beef canned in half-gallon jars with gravy and onions. Neat 1" squares so tender and tasty, you never needed a knife—a fork would break the meat apart. It was served with mashed potatoes and preacher peas. This meat, of course, you could keep all summer. Corned beef or salt-cured brisket of beef was also made and sliced cold in summer.

We wrapped one hindquarter of beef in a clean sheet and stored it in the stone granary basement where it stayed cool until late spring. This would be the last of the fresh meat to be eaten usually into April and even early May. There was no finer steak ever eaten than this juicy, extremely tender, well "seasoned" steak. A fork was all you needed to break apart a good steak or swiss steak, even if the piece was a little sinewy.

Our next favorite was dried beef. It was a special treat we ate in July and August during haying and the cutting and shocking of grain. It had to be shaved extremely fine to be good. We sat in the shade and ate a lunch of fresh home-baked bread with sweet butter, as two dogs and seven cats watched. Mutt, our rat terrier, could usually wheedle a small piece of dried beef from Bob. Jack, the collie, got only a crust of bread. We'd wash the sandwiches down with home-made root beer, just pulled off the snow in the cistern. This was manna from heaven and liquid ambrosia, a drink of the gods. On a hot day, I'd bet that Bacchus, the Roman god of wine, would willingly trade 10 barrels of his brew for one glass of our home-made root beer. Lunch was topped off with just-baked, golden yellow cake with black walnuts and half an inch of boiled frosting which was soft, sweet and creamy, made with brown sugar and lots of vanilla. Please beam me back, Scotty, I'm going crazy!

It was difficult for Mother to get her kitchen knives sharpened until she told Dad, "No more dried beef until my knives are sharpened." Dad would say, "Come on, Milton. Turn the grindstone. Let's get those knives sharpened!" Voila! Sharp knives.

Imagine how many hours of turning, cutting, stirring—with aching muscles and headaches—it took my mother to handle the food preparation for a family of ten. Alone, she did more work in January than many a woman does all year, nowadays!

Grinding meat required a good deal of exertion.

I was interested when Ed Sjostrum, our Maiden Rock neighbor, showed me this rather amusing description from an unidentified old newspaper clipping:

When we grind sausage, we use our auto to turn the grinder. We brace the car so it will be perfectly steady, then jack up the rear wheels and place the sausage-mill by the jacked-up wheels. Be sure to have the shaft of the grinder in line with axle of auto. We put the grinder on blocks so a receptacle can be placed to catch the sausage. With binder twine we tie the handle of the grinder to the spoke of wheel. Have a person sit on each end of board to which grinder is attached, then start the motor, putting it in second gear. In this way meat from seven good-sized hogs can be ground in a half-hour or less.

Floy Bates, Mo.

Firewood, It Heats You Many Times

With the severe cold of January behind us, it was time to go into the woods to cut firewood. If handling meat was labor intensive, getting wood from the tree to the fire was even more so. It required 12 to 14 separate operations:

1. Cut the tree down with a 2-man crosscut saw.

2. Trim off and pile branches.

3. Large logs, some up to 3' in diameter, 60' to 70' in height, were drilled and filled with black powder, a fuse and fragments of crushed brick. This was carefully tamped in using a metal rod to hold the powder secure when it was ignited.

4. Logs split in half lengthwise would be further reduced in size with wedges and a splitting maul.

5. Split logs, smaller diameter logs and branches were pulled down the steeper hillsides to a lower level so they could be more easily reached by an open-ended sleigh. It was my job to ride a horse up and down the slippery hill all day.

6. These worked-up pieces were sawn into lengths, so two men could lift them onto the sleigh. The smaller trees were cut 8' to 10'. More slender branches could be cut 12' to 14' long. The sleigh load of firewood material was hauled back to the farm building area. It was an adrenaline rush coming down the hill road with a load of logs and the team going full out!

7. While unloading the sleigh, we piled logs in a row 5' to 6' high. We placed the heaviest cuts on the bottom. The pile often extended 30' or more.

8. In March, we assembled a crew of 6 or 7 men to saw the long pieces into firewood. Usually a neighbor had a saw rig which could be attached to the motor of a tractor. Power from the tractor was transmitted to the saw by two pulleys and a belt. A crew of three or four men working together lifted and carried a log to the saw and held it steadily while the saw cut a 16" section from one end. Another man on the opposite side, threw the cut pieces onto a nearby pile. The crew worked in unison to move the log away, forward and back into the saw for another 16" cut. This was heavy work, especially throwing the firewood. The men changed positions every hour.

Firewood was a constant need. An old saying was "heating with firewood heated you many times" as it was processed and moved to be burnt. Goodhue County Historical Society Photo.

It was extremely important the men worked in unison to prevent the saw from pinching or binding. The owner, alert to the steady sound of the saw, was quick to detect any whining, indicating the logs were not handled correctly. For example, if a log was held too loosely or allowed to torque against the blade it could damage the valuable equipment or worker. The saw would need to be sharpened often by hand filing, depending on the amount of dirt on the logs.

Usually the whole process took two days. Remember, after the men finished a hard day processing firewood, they went home to their regular daily farm chores!

9. In April, the firewood would be further separated with the tough knotty pieces for the furnace and the straight-grained ones split for our cooking stoves.

10. The furnace wood was piled so it would dry better.

Buzz Saw Sled—A buzz saw was used to cut longer lengths into 16" pieces. It was extremely important that the men worked in unison to prevent the saw from pinching or binding. Goodhue County Historical Society Photo.

Clearing Land, Blowing Up Stumps

by son Tom Hayman

My father Milton Hayman carried his childhood work ethic and learnings along with him throughout his life. When he was about 40 and I was about 15, my parents bought a farm south of Minneapolis that had, in part, five acres of partially cleared land. It would have made sense to hire a D8 Cat to come in and push out all the stumps in a day or two and pile up all the wood and burn it. However, that is not the way it was done on the Hayman farm in Hay Creek.

Dad had a goal of clearing the five acres and putting it into tillable land that did not include mechanization. It did, however, involve leather gloves, a six-foot-long oak-handled spade, shovels, dynamite and two years of work! We worked spring, summer and fall piling logs and slash into piles that were twelve feet high.

Sometimes these piles were around stumps to burn them out, but there were many, many more stumps. So, much of the time was spent on our hands and knees digging holes under the center of stumps. This meant finding an opening between the roots of the stump and using the spade to loosen the soil and pull the dirt out by hand. The objective was to create a cavity under the stump large enough to pack in the sticks of dynamite. The rule of thumb was one stick of dynamite per inch of stump. A ten-inch stump required digging a cavity that we could stuff in ten 2" x 9" sticks of dynamite.

We would chop and dig through roots and dirt to prepare five stumps. The most dangerous part was putting the little metal blasting cap on the end of the fuse and then inserting it into one of the sticks of dynamite that we had previously punctured with a hole. We put this in the hole in the ground with the other sticks of dynamite and then packed the hole with dirt. It was critical to pack it tight so the explosion did not just blow out one side and leave the stump in place. We would use punks to light the fuses. Dad would light three and I would light the other two. We would run like heck and take shelter behind the two big white silos and listen. Boom! Boom! Boom! Boom! And then we would look at each other and say did you hear five? Inevitably, two went at the same time, but we waited a long time to assess and then carefully walked back to see if we could see the five holes.

The biggest part of the project was collecting the parts of the stump and roots. These five

An oak spud was used to create a cavity under a stump that was large enough to pack in the sticks of dynamite. The rule of thumb was one stick of dynamite per inch of stump!

acres were surrounded by fields on three sides. We then had to drag the heavy wet roots and wood back and stack it up on one of the many piles. We thought we were safe taking shelter behind the silos but eventually noted that there were many pieces that flew up and landed inside the topless silos!

We blew up over 200 stumps and purchased over 20 cases (144 sticks each) of dynamite. The big event was the 24-inch stump: what a job to pack in the dynamite and what an explosion! It was exhausting, dirty work, but the grand fires into the evenings and the feeling of progress made it all worthwhile. I felt I learned a lot about the determination and hard work that was required to grow up on the farm in the '30s and '40s. I have only in more recent years come to fully appreciate the experience, its impacts on me and the desire to share it.

11. In October, firewood was moved from the outdoor piles, with the split wood going into the woodshed and the blocks going into the basement of our house.

12. The split wood was carried from the woodshed into the house as needed and piled in a wood box—that was most certainly my job.

13. Stoves and the furnace had to be constantly tended, adding wood to keep fires going.

14. Stoves needed to be regularly cleaned for efficient operation. The ashes were taken out and used for various purposes, such as soap-making, to improve traction on slippery roads and in the garden during summer months to control garden pests.

An old saying was "heating with firewood heated you many times!"

Anyone for a propane tank, a natural gas hookup or electric heat?

Hayman Farm photo circa 1867. Note the lack of woods on the hillsides.

Winter Chores

During the four winter months, a constant routine went on uninterrupted. We'd milk the cows by hand then carry the milk to the house to be separated. Afterwards, we carried the skim milk back to the barn to feed the calves. We fed the cows—twice in the barn and once outside each day. Once a day we'd clean the cow barn with a cable carrier. We'd take the sleigh and horses and use a fork to spread manure on the fields. With the same fork, we'd dig straw for bedding from a straw pile. This often took place in the wind or during a snowstorm.

Regardless of the weather, all our animals needed water. Our large cement tank was boarded up in late fall and surrounded with packed straw. A crescent-shaped, wood-burning water heater was installed to heat the water from December to March. Starting the fire could be fun. We'd splash gasoline onto the wood, toss in a match and *whoosh!* long plumes of flame would shoot out.

Some straw was stored in the loft of the calf barn. Usually, this was done on a nice day and required 3 or 4 hay rack loads. Our cows were also fed ground corn and oats and, in the evening, mangels, a very large beet-like root, that was cut up and placed on top of their ground feed.

In January, grinding feed for cows and hogs was a great winter "sport." We hauled grain from the granary to the feed mill and then tried to start our old Titan tractor. If it would not start, we'd light a fire under it. If it still wouldn't start, we'd drain the water out of the block, go to the house to get fresh hot water and pour it in the radiator. This whole process could take as long as several hours just to get the tractor started. We fed grain very slowly into an old burr mill. We carried corn from the corn crib with a bushel basket on our shoulders and fed it into the burr mill. Then the two feeds were blended and carried to feed barrels in all our barns. This was hard, back-breaking work.

The same routine went for hogs, chickens, calves, steers and horses that were fed twice a day. Their pens and stalls were cleaned once a week.

Occasionally, our hogs got a special treat of steamed hot cooked rye and old potatoes from the cook shanty where water, fire and a large iron kettle were available. In summer we watched the bald-faced hornets chewing on the cottonwood boards. They'd roll up fine strips of wood which they chewed and used to make paper nests high up in the trees. The sides of the shed were ridged with grooves made by these hornets.

Digging manure out of the calf and steer pens was another real backbreaker. Bob or the hired man often broke fork handles. Dad finally tired of replacing handles and said, "Anyone breaking a handle from now on will have to put a new one in themselves." After that, fewer handles were broken. Dad's other famous saying regarding wild game was, "You shoot it, you clean and eat it."

The manure carrier was suspended from rafters and went down the middle. Manure from the gutters was shoveled into it. St. Louis County Historical Society Photo.

Each winter our 4 or 5 horses were fed timothy hay and no oats, unless they worked all day. In summer, they worked hard, long days and usually received two meals of oats. Sometimes it was hard to get them back into the barn after they had a few days off, but putting oats in their feed box solved that problem. Dick was our smartest horse. He was a good worker. He was black with white socks. He'd open the horse-barn door by using his nose to slide the bolt back. Cap, one of our hired men, got Dick to chew snuff and he learned to love it. We'd ask Dick if he wanted snuff and he'd sneeze. Pete, a white horse, was a perfect reincarnation of Rozinante, Cervantes' Bag of Bones.

Gim, my grandmother, was a source of common good sense. Mid-March she'd say, "Charles, the snow is going. It's time to fill the cistern." The cistern, when packed with snow, was our refrigerator. Its main purpose was to store cream for 2 to 3 days until it was taken to be sold in Red Wing. It also preserved our family's milk, butter, asparagus and root beer for family use. Cream was kept in 'shotgun cans', so named because of their shape. They were a 10" cylinder 30" high with a loose-fitting metal cover that kept anything from falling in — like cow manure!

Our cistern was about 10' in diameter and 18' deep and was lined with several coats of cement. Each spring it had to be pumped out. In early years this was done by hand, but with the advent of electricity in the late 1930s, a pump jack with an electric motor was used. Someone had to crawl down a ladder to clean out the last foot of water and dirt and wash it out with clean water. Then a grain box was put on a sleigh to carry snow from the last large snow drifts. This usually took 2 days.

The wagon boxes were taken off of the sleighs and put on wheels for the summer. The sleighs were broken down and stacked in our blacksmith shop.

During April, manure was spread over our fields before spring plowing. The manure piles near the cow barn were huge and partly frozen. This made loading the manure spreader very challenging work. Three horses would pull the spreader so we didn't have to spread it with a hand fork. The horse manure pile was easier because the ammonia it produced made it hot. Pig manure smelled awful!

As a child, it was fun swinging hand over hand along the manure cable until dropping onto the manure pile at the end. This served me well in my freshman gym class. The coach made everyone go hand over hand around the gym hanging onto a balcony rail about 10' off the floor. I was the only one to go along all three sides. During my high school years, this was my only sports fame.

April was grain-cleaning time. We'd run grain through a fanning mill to blow out the weed seeds. It was turned by hand until electricity came and that saved a lot of hard back work. Seed corn was shelled by hand and the cobs were saved for use in the smokehouse.

Manure carrier: "It was fun swinging hand over hand along the manure cable until dropping onto the manure pile at the end."

Springtime

Spring was when we castrated calves and hogs. We'd catch a hog, stuff the head in a nail barrel and wash the testicles before removing its "pig hood." Jack, our dog, stood there and caught every pair that was thrown out the door. The wound was treated with stock dip and the pig placed in a clean pen with fresh straw to heal for 2 or 3 days. Young calves also had to be dehorned. It was a nasty, bloody job but necessary for the safety of both humans and animals.

Wilbur and Bob with crocuses at the sand hill overlook which was across the valley. Note: See photo on the following page to the left of the V for Victory symbol for the location of the sandhill overlook.

By the end of March or early April, depending on the arrival of spring-like weather, the garden's hot bed was started. A load of steaming horse manure was hauled into the yard and forked into a 6' x 9' bed, 16" deep. A frame was placed around it and several inches of black soil were shoveled on top. Dad laid three old storm windows side by side across the frame to hold the heat in.

After a few days, the earth inside would warm from the manure and be ready for seed planting. Once prepared, Gim would plant and then keep an eye on the hot bed. Certain jobs Gim liked, and Mom was more than happy to get her out from under foot! Gim always planted early and late tomatoes, cabbage, peppers, cauliflower, celery and some flowers. One-sixth of the hot bed was planted to leaf lettuce and radishes for early eating. The hot bed had to be carefully watched, watered and vented on sunny days to let out excess heat. When plants were 4" to 6" high, they were transplanted into our big garden. In fall, the hot bed was dug out and made ready for the next spring.

According to Bob, Gim grew hops on octagonal chicken wire behind a corn crib, to make "home brew beer." Hops—small, cone-shaped catkins that grew from the flowers—were gathered and dried. Some people bought malt, but Gim made her own by soaking barley and then allowing it to sprout. As the barley sprouted, the starch changed to sugar. Gim would chew the sprouts to taste the sweetness. At just the right time, when the sprouts were still quite small, she'd roast the barley and then crush it to better release the sugar. This is how it became malt.

As the malt was cooked, a small bag of hops was suspended in the liquid to add flavor. It was known as "wort" when the mixture cooled. Then it was strained and placed in a 60-gallon crock. Yeast was added to start fermentation. Gim watched the color and skimmed off the foam. After several days, the fermenting was nearly done. Sometimes a little caramel was added to improve the color before her brew was siphoned into bottles. Wilbur added a teaspoon of sugar to each bottle to continue the fermentation and give the beer a "head." Three to four days later, it was ready to drink.

Willy loved to tell his bottling story. He'd cap the beer bottles after Gim filled them. She used a 4' hose. One end was in the tank of brew and she'd suck on the other end to start the flow. She'd quickly insert the end into a bottle. When filled, she'd pinch the end of the hose, tip it up to drain and start the process again. Willy said he could start the flow with one suck, but Gim took three. She secretly drank the raw beer!

Everyone said Gim made the best homebrew around. In the evening, Cap, our hired man, would call me over to the big wooden rocking chair where he sat, and quietly say, "Run downstairs and get a bottle of beer." I'd look at Gim for a nod of approval and then take off. The big quart bottles provided a glass for Cap ("Big Bozo"), Gim, Dad and a

Corn Planting Stories
by Nephew Niles Deden

Like all retired farmers, Wilbur liked to sit at the kitchen table, look out the windows and watch the farm. When I joined him one day, Wilbur told me one of my favorite stories.

He had a small 245 Massey tractor that he used to pull a 4-row corn planter that used dry starter fertilizer. He had to shovel the fertilizer from a wagon into the hoppers on the corn planter, which took a lot of time and was a lot of work. He was proud that one year he really busted his hump and got that 23-acre field planted in just one long day. He and I were sitting at his table drinking coffee and watching Tom Bowe plant that field with a 12-row corn planter and liquid fertilizer. Tom planted the field in just under two hours. Wilbur never told that story again. Sad.

At some point, the short corn rows, caused by the road to the sand hill, became a nuisance. The road was eliminated and we just drove through the field. The combined field now measures 49.41 acres. I kind of know how Wilbur felt. The current renter plants the whole 50 acres in less than two hours and his rows are perfectly straight, thanks to GPS.

Note the corn planted so it could be cultivated in two different directions and the V for Victory on the Sand Hill.

In 2000, planting corn with a 12 row corn planter and liquid fertilizer.

small one, the size of a pimento cream cheese glass, for "Little Bozo". That was me. "Big Bozo" and "Little Bozo" were the waggish names we called each other.

Spring was the time mother set clucks, each on 12-15 eggs, to hatch baby chicks. After hatching, they were placed in little tin houses on the lawn and fed fine feed, bread crumbs and special water with a red pill dissolved in it to prevent disease.

The end of April was plow, plow, plow. We used a five-horse hitch to pull a 2-bottom, 16" sulky plow, preparing the corn ground where manure was recently spread. Grain ground was always plowed late in the fall. In spring it was worked with a spring tooth then dragged with a 5-section drag using four horses to break up the soil and set back weeds. Grain was drilled into the soil with a 7' drill. Dad used four tall, thin sticks about 8' long with a flag on top to act as guides across a large field, so he didn't miss, or overlap and waste precious hay or clover seeds.

Later a 10' grain drill with two seed boxes was used. The larger box held grain. The smaller box held timothy, red clover and later, alfalfa. Once the grain was harvested, the young hay plants that had grown in their shade remained and were cut for hay for the next two years.

In earlier times, farmers seeded fields with a hand spreader. This was a bag of seeds with a flywheel that was turned to broadcast seeds over a wide area. Now and then, we'd use one to spread new grass seed on recently disturbed areas such as ravines, dams and roadsides.

A week after planting, we dragged the fields to cover the seeds and kill small weeds that sprouted. The drag was so wide, it often was broken apart before it could be hauled on a wagon from one field to another.

Bob usually planted corn with a 2-row planter. Before he began the process, he'd unroll a wire the length of the field with knots every 36". When the planter hit the knot, it deposited 3 to 4 kernels of corn. The end stake had to be moved 36" every round and kept in a straight line. This was important, because there were no herbicides and the fields would be cultivated in both directions, using a horse-drawn two-row cultivator. This was a very tedious job. The 40 to 60 acres of corn had to be cultivated three and sometimes four times each summer. We cultivated the end of May, mid-June, first of July, and later in the summer. Corn was supposed to be "knee-high by the 4th of July."

For the women of our family, May was the time to air and beat mattresses in the sun, and wash and store away flannel sheets and winter clothes. Woolen clothes were washed outside in a very flammable dry-cleaning fluid. All clothes were packed away in the linen chest with ample mothballs. In the fall, when we first wore them again, we'd smell up the whole church (a child's great concern), but then, other parishioners also smelled of mothballs. It was a better smell than sweat!

A Sunday afternoon springtime diversion was crossing the valley to the sand hill to pick the first crocuses (pasque flowers). Sometimes my sisters would come along and, once in a great while, my mother would join us. Violets grew on the other hill in the western hog pasture. A few yellow lady slippers grew up in the hollow west of Sip's place.

Dora with Adeline and Edith. "For the women in our family, May was the time to air and beat mattresses in the sun, and wash and store flannel sheets and winter clothes."

A Full Potato Bin

To provide all the vegetables and potatoes needed for a large family, we'd plow 2 ½ acres to plant. The field was marked with a horse-drawn device of wood with runners underneath, 30" apart, and a pole on one side to mark the return trip back across the field. The pole was switched from one side to the other every time we crossed the plot. When the ground was soft this was great for planting sweet corn and navy beans. It took just one swipe of the hoe and our seeds got planted.

Potato rows were plowed open with a V-plow. Then the fun of planting two acres of potatoes by hand began. Last year's leftover potatoes were cut into 3 to 5 pieces. We walked along the row with a pail of "seed potatoes" and dropped them 12" apart, if possible with an "eye", or sprout end, facing up. If we failed, we didn't bother to take time to bend down and turn over the seed potato. When the potatoes were all planted, they were covered by using a corn cultivator. The center shovel was turned to throw soil inward and an iron drag followed cross-ways to complete filling the trough. Then they were dragged once more to kill any small weeds just coming up. In June and July they were cultivated with a corn cultivator, then later with one horse and a garden cultivator. As the vines grew, this cultivator would shove them aside. The real fun began in July or early August when they needed hand-hoeing!

In early October, the potatoes were plowed out with a V-plow and then dug out of the loose soil by hand using a small four-tined, curved rake with a short wooden handle. After many days, many pails of potatoes filled many grain boxes full of potatoes. Some went into a large bin, 6' x 8' by 6' high, in the basement of the house. This was our winter and spring supply.

The rest were piled on the granary floor to be hand-culled and sacked for sale in Red Wing.

Dad cut the back off of an old Studebaker and turned it into a truck. He loaded it with sacks of potatoes and he went door to door to sell them in Red Wing. Many years he sold potatoes to the same people. He carried the sacks into their basements and filled their potato bins. I don't know what price he got, but I remember it wasn't very much. Bob said they sold some for 25 cents a bushel. One dry, bad growing year, he got $1.50 a bushel.

We ate potatoes twice a day. Every morning Gim would peel a dishpan full of potatoes to cook. She boiled them for the noon meal and fried them for the evening meal. What was left over, the dogs and cats ate! Feeding a family of nine or ten took a lot of potatoes!

Mangles were planted near the potatoes, beans and sweet corn. They were easy to plant in the marked rows. Later they had to be thinned, weeded and hoed. Just before frost in October they were pulled, trimmed and hauled into the barn in the manure carrier and stored under the stairs. In a good season they grew very large, 7" diameter, 30" long. They were red and yellowish-white in color. Their food value for cows was questionable, but our cows liked them. It could have been an idea from some university farm-campus expert who wrote a thesis on the subject.

Gim with her grandchildren, Robert, Edith, Adeline and Wilbur. Milt arrived on the scene three years later.

Tree Forts and Caves

During the diversified farming of the 1930s Depression Era, we occasionally got time off from work on rainy days or between jobs or when Dad went to Red Wing. To escape from the jobs of the day, such as cutting weeds, hoeing potatoes or gardening, Willie and Bob would climb onto the platform high up on the old windmill, lay flat and hide. Dad would holler for them but they wouldn't answer. Once he drove out the driveway, they'd climb down and head for the hills, literally, either the sand hill across the valley or the one behind our barn.

Hayman family circa 1927. Milt was born in 1928.

With hammer, nails, hatchet, or ax, they'd headed out. Their intended project was a tree house high up in the crotch of a giant burr oak. The tree was tough as nails because it grew in rock on the south side of the hill. The tree house was about 25' above the ground, probably 5' x 7' and 5' high with a pitched roof. Lumber was precious. Very little was available. If any was left over from a farm building project, a building, wagon or gate, it was too far to carry across a valley and up a bluff. However, my brothers were inventive and determined. Their tree house was made entirely from young slender oak trees or oak branches 1 ½" to 2" in diameter that had been killed by a fire that swept across the hillside during those drought-ridden years. Fire greatly aided the survival of the bed of crocuses on the lower hill by setting back any invading trees or shrubs and returning nutrients to the soil.

It's hard to imagine the number of days it took to cut all those trees, cut them to length and pull them up into the huge oak. Perseverance prevailed and somehow they "appropriated" tar paper for the roof. I can hear it all now: Dad, "Where'd that tar paper go?" Brothers, "I don't know." The less words the better, so you can't get trapped in them.

Dad hung a strap over an old gun above the door and often used it on my brothers, sometimes either with or without cause. He must have agreed with Butler, "Their wickedness at birth was but very imperfectly wiped out at Baptism." As for me, I feared Dad decidedly more than I feared the devil. He had only to look at the strap to paralyze me white with fear. So much for loving relationships.

The fort sported a small deck-like, loggia about a foot wide under one side of the roof. With no railing, there was no way I could be induced to crawl out on it!

Figuring the girls would eventually find our fort, we went to great lengths to make it hard to gain access to it. About 18' from the great oak was a smaller one about 10" in diameter. With our arms and legs clamped around it, it was easy for us boys to shimmy up that tree. We knew very well, few girls—with the exception of Mugs Broze—could accomplish this.

About 12' up the smaller tree we built a swinging suspension bridge that went across to the great oak. Again, we used 2" sticks, interwoven with smooth wire and built the floor of the bridge, about 18" wide. We secured it to both ends of the trees. A wire handrail on each side had wire dropping to the floor every 30". There may be girls that can shimmy up trees, but not one in a hundred would walk across a swaying bridge 18' to 24' above the ground. Right? Girls might find it, but never assault it. (My, how things with girls changed, 10 years later!).

We kept a wood stick ladder lying on the bridge so only one person had to climb up and let the ladder down. A ladder made it easier to bring other materials up.

Of course, our sisters figured something was in the wind when the boys disappeared across the valley. They'd get together and try to locate our fort, but we kept it a secret by never entering the woods from the same spot.

Willy and Bob always had a pretty good idea of when Dad would return home. When he drove into the yard, he always found them energetically at work, hoeing or cutting weeds with a scythe. What parent could scold offspring for working so diligently?

If my wits are well-caulked, I believe my brothers gave up their aerie pursuits and next went underground. Mother would have told them they were destined for Hell if they did not go to church, so they decided a little first-hand knowledge of Dantes' realm would later keep them in good stead, at least on the first Level.

Off the hill road, just below the last sharp rise where the team came out of the woods, was 80 acres of farmland. My brothers shoveled out a 16" hole in the bank and dug a tunnel about 4' long before they hollowed out a room about 4 x 5 feet, 5 feet high.

"The tree house was made entirely from young slender oak trees or oak branches 1½" to 2" in diameter that had been killed by a fire that swept across the hillside during those drought-ridden years."

This time they found use for their little brother. I was sworn to secrecy and upon threats of pain of death or at least bodily mutilation if I told anyone of the location of the cave. I was small enough to rapidly and efficiently pull a little two-wheeled wagon full of dirt out of the tunnel. I dumped the dirt in a ditch about 20' into the woods. I was ecstatic, ready to bust with importance, as I worked with my older brothers and kept an important secret from my sisters and the Broze girls.

After every dig they closed the hole with a wooden door, covered it with dirt and piled some dead branches on top. They'd walk off to the side, then down to the hill road and leave no visible evidence of the location. Many times, the girls walked up and down the hill road looking for our cave, but they never found it.

In the cave, light was required, and candles slowly disappeared from our house. We built wood stools for added comfort. The cave was only about 300 yards from the hill orchard that had a dozen or more apple trees. The first to ripen was the white and soft "Snow Apple." It was followed by Dutchess, Whitney crabs, Wealthy, Melindas and finally, the Greenings, which we picked before the last big frost. In fall, one of my jobs was to take a horse and stone boat up to the orchard and gather all the downed, windfall apples and haul them to the pigs. Those curly-tailed little buggers loved 'em.

Hayman children dressed to go out.

Later on, we dug another tunnel with a smaller back room. The hill sloped toward the ditch and we had to dig around box elder roots. Then after a strong summer storm, tragedy occurred. Water followed the tree roots and flooded our cave and left dirt in the second room. It was decision time. We opened the whole back room ceiling and timbered the roof with small trees. We replaced the dirt and covered it with branches to avoid detection from "girl" enemies. Forts are designed by boys to fight off imaginary enemies. We used slingshots, javelins (pointed sticks), rocks, etc. This was a place "girls" could not find or get into. Ours was a complete world, free from girls — and that included my two sisters, the two Broze girls, and any other female friends or rellies that might chance to visit.

Our last retreat was a tower fort built on the west side of the sand hill in an aspen grove, near a large oak. By then, Willie and Bob were in high school. It was small, palisade-type, 3' x 3' inside diameter, about 14' high. Four corner posts were set into the ground and between them 6" aspens stood upright, stabilized on the inside with horizontal boards. One corner was designed with a door that locked on the inside. We'd crawled up the inside to a platform 3' below the top. A hole was left in one corner so we could get up and onto the platform. There were no seats because we were out-growing this play.

These construction feats were accomplished in fits and spurts, because farming required year-round endeavor to keep food in the paunch and clothes on our backs.

Make Hay While The Sun Shines

June, July and September were continuous rounds of haying. In the Depression years we cut meadow hay, June grass, switchgrass, timothy and a little alsike white clover. It was a tremendous challenge cutting it after a heavy rain flooded the valley and deposited mud, sticks and even logs. Flooded haygrounds produced hay that was dirty. The cows did not like dirty, dusty hay but sometimes it got damp and fermented into a kind of silage that our cows loved.

In the later years we grew timothy and red and white clover that provided more nourishment. Finally, alfalfa became the crop of choice because it could provide as many as three cuttings and was easier to stack into the bins.

Meadow hay was cut with a two-horse mower with a 5' sickle blade that needed to be sharpened twice a day if the hay was dirty. While cutting, we'd see red-winged blackbird nests in the yellow dock and would try to avoid cutting them. We'd lift the mower to avoid meadowlarks nesting on the ground and the bobolink nests in the weeds. The parent birds would flutter around helplessly, issuing distress calls. Try as we might, some nests were always lost. Nests suffered many threats. Once the hay was cut, the raccoon could find them more easily. Later they might be hit by a tedder or a dump rake.

Tedding was done after a rain to stir or turn the hay and help it dry. Later, the dump rake dragged hay into rows so it could be hand-pitched onto a hay rack. Chaff would fall down our necks, mix with our sweat and cause incessant itching. Loads of hay were taken to the hay shed to be divided into four bins. Hay was pulled off the wagon with a hay fork, ropes and pulleys and was pulled up by a boy and a horse in the back of the shed.

Getting meadow hay into a bin was sometimes difficult, especially if it had a large quantity of June grass, which made it very slippery. The set fork would just pull out a little clump of hay requiring the rope fork to be pulled back to the wagon and then reset. Sometimes it was just easier to fork off the bottom of the wagon into an empty bin.

Red and white clover and timothy went into the old slant roof barn where it was hard to mow (pronounced *mou*) hay. Usually, in July, it was hotter than the 12th level of Hell when we shoved large masses of hay to the side under the roof. After unloading two wagons under such conditions, we'd head for the cow tank and drink about a gallon of water before holding our heads under the faucet to cool down. If it was 100 degrees outside, it was 120 degrees under that roof. That's when lunch, with

Loading hay with a rear mounted hay loader. Goodhue County Historical Society Photo.

Moving hay from wagon to hay stacks for storage. The conical shape shed water and snow. Note the fly net on the horse harness. Goodhue County Historical Society Photo.

The Hayman hay shed had a large fork that was connected with pulleys that was used to unload a hay wagon. Other equipment was stored under the lean-to roof.

snow-cold root beer was like manna from Heaven and liquid ambrosia from the gods.

Usually the calf barn loft was filled with good quality hay to start them thinking cow life was beautiful. The horse loft got the poorest and toughest timothy hay. Both lofts were forked in by hand and mounded inside. Later we put in a load or two of very tender September alfalfa for the hogs and chickens.

Some years we'd leave a couple of acres of second-cut red clover and have it threshed for seed and haul it to a neighbor where a threshing machine was set up.

Modernization came very slowly to "Willow Bush Farm," but it did come. First with a side-delivery rake and a Minnesota hay loader of rope and slats that was returned to the equipment dealership because fine meadow hay fell through the cracks. Later, we purchased a push type that worked well. At first the horses were afraid of the noise, panicked and buried the men in the back who were loading hay. Many swear words were sent forth, mostly referring to the Lad Upstairs and a construction built to store water and create lakes.

Hauling hay was exciting when we came down a hill, especially standing on pile 8' high or more. If the wagon wheel hit a gopher mound, the wagon box could tip to one side. A number of times we were thrown off and had to pick ourselves up off the ground but we climbed right back on.

A large fork connected to a rope with pulleys was used to unload the hay wagons. One man on the wagon "set" the fork down into the hay and then lifted two latches to keep the hay from falling out. The load was lifted up and over into the mow. One of the men in the mow had a long pole he used to push the load that caused it to swing. At just the right second, as the load was swinging over the pile, he'd yell, "Pull!" The man on the wagon would pull a cord and release the hay. Any hesitation and the load landed in the wrong spot and had to be forked by hand. More swear words!

Alfalfa was easy to unload, with maybe six sets of the hay fork, but was difficult to mow back under the roof. The stems and leaves were one tangled mass, and God help the poor bastard who had to dig it out in January. There goes another vertebra.

Hay "was cut with a two-horse, ground powered mower with a 5' sickle bar that needed to be sharpened twice a day." Fillmore County Historical Society Photo.

Life or Death on the Hill Road
by Nephew Dan Hayman

We often had hay fields on "the hill" and "in the valley". Hill hay dried faster because there was less morning dew and had more drying winds and therefore usually produced superior quality hay. The problem was getting down the steep hill road without losing the load or getting into more serious trouble. I usually drove the tractor and Dad (Wilbur) loaded bales on the wagon.

When time permitted, we would use twine from broken bales to tie the top front bales together and secure them to bales further back to use more of the total mass of the load to hold the front bales in place. This worked if you didn't hit a rock or a hole on the way down the hill road when you could lose most of the load which was harder to restack on the steep hillside and required leaving some bales by the wayside to be retrieved later.

One time it started to pour rain while we were baling hay and Dad drove the load down the muddy hill road, lost his brakes on the slippery hill road and skidded out of control most of the way down. Luckily no one got injured or killed.

The hill road was equally challenging during the fall when corn was harvested and road conditions were less than ideal—muddy, icy or snow-covered.

Threshing Crew

By the end of July, the winter wheat would be ripe. We'd pull the binder out of the barn where it had been stored and was covered with fodder blown in from corn shredding.

1. First we'd assemble the front carrying wheel
2. Then put the canvas aprons on
3. Install two rolls of Minnesota prison-made twine and thread it into the knotter
4. We'd grease and oil gears and pulleys
5. Then sharpen the 8' scythe
6. We'd harness four horses and hitch them to binder and go to the first field. We had to change the two-wheel transport to the side or front for cutting. This was no easy job as everything was very heavy.

We'd cut, cut, cut. First Bob, then Willy, while the rest of us would shock the bundles in straight rows so the bundle teams could later on quickly and easily load the bundles. A shock was a group of bundles tipped together. We'd grab one bundle in each hand and then slam the butts into the ground. We'd add four more bundles on each side and sometimes—with wheat or rye—an extra bundle was set at the middle of each side. Some farmers added a bundle as a cap to shed rain while waiting for the thresher.

Next we'd cut spring wheat that was mixed with oats, then straight oats, then barley with shorter, nasty beards. One year I pulled an inch-long festering barley beard out of my belly button. The barbs kept working it deeper and deeper.

Shocks had to be well-built or else a heavy summer storm could knock them down. Sometimes they had to be re-shocked or the grain would sprout and spoil. There could be more haying as we waited for the grain to dry. Certainly there was no lack of work.

We'd sweep out and repair all the grain bins. There were six on the first floor, three or four upstairs. We'd cut tin to nail over mouse holes, patch grain sacks, stamp "C. W. Hayman" on each one so not to be lost if mixed up or borrowed. The hill road and ditch crossings were repaired with a scoop and team of horses.

During late August into early September, we'd experience an endless round of threshing, the process of separating the grain from the cut stalks with our neighbors, the Hawkinsons, Horns, Langhans, Kolshorns. One year we'd start at one end of the neighborhood and then the other end the next year. Some smaller farms complained that it took too long to get to them, so they did two days at each farm and then came back to finish. This created a lot of moving for Joe Zignigo, the owner of the threshing machine.

Threshing was a neighborhood affair that usually took a crew of 12 to 15. One man driving his own horses and wagon was called a bundle team. Usually 6 bundle teams worked to pick up grain bundles from the fields. The shocks were opened and bundles placed on their wagons in two rows, lengthwise, grain heads to the center. Each man loaded his own wagon until it became too high. Then a field pitcher

A binder cut grain and bound the cut grain into bundles. Goodhue County Historical Society Photo.

helped by tossing bundles up so the man could continue stacking and tapering the load inward to make it more stable. Bob liked that job because it was away from the noise and dirt of the machine.

The loaded wagon was driven to the threshing machine and unloaded. The bundles were placed head first on the "apron." This was a continuous conveyor-type belt of wood slats and chain. It had knives that cut the strings on the bundles. Bundles were crushed in between a stationary metal plate with teeth projecting upward and meshed with teeth on a rotating cylinder above. Grain, chaff and straw fell below onto a horizontal auger. It was moved to the side, then augered up to a mechanism where it was reworked, shaken and sifted until the grain was clean. The straw and chaff was blown by a high-speed fan onto a nearby straw pile 15' to 20' high. The straw would be used for animal bedding during the winter months.

Dad stacked straw and kept the top of the pile even and tapered. I tended the blower by constantly turning the angle and raising the hood to blow the straw to the back of the pile. A good blower tender made the job easier for the stacker.

Two men on a grain wagon bed tended the grain that went into a bucket that weighed and counted each half bushel. They alternated sacking the grain as it flowed through a spout, pulling the sacks forward and leaning them, untied, against the front of the wagon. As the wagon filled with a "Giddyup," or "Whoa," the horses moved the wagon forward. The loaded grain wagon headed to the granary to empty the sacks into the bins. The front of the bin was open so they could walk in. As grain piled up, boards were added across the opening. A 2' x 12' plank formed a ramp for access. As the bin filled, a third man shoveled the grain to the back corners. Unloading the grain sacks in granaries became very hard work when the bin was full and high or the sacks had to be carried to the upstairs bins. Oats were lighter, but wheat and rye were very heavy.

A bundle wagon moved the bundles of grain from the field to the threshing site, circa 1900. Goodhue County Historical Society Photo.

Joe owned the thresher and a large tractor. All the equipment was powered by the main drive of the tractor. Two men could constantly pitch in bundles if they were dry and entered the machine heads first. In rainy, wet years the butts would be wet, green and sprouted, and the cylinder would howl as the bundles passed through. If a man got ornery, he might throw in 2 or 3 together or sideways, or one on top of the other. This would plug the head and throw off the belt to the tractor pulley.

It could take Joe half an hour to unplug the machine and put the belt back, all the while swearing at the machine and at the man who plugged it. This down time allowed men on the bundle team to sit and rest. Arnold Langhans was a great one for doing this but usually only after his farm had been threshed. Joe knew this and raised hell with him.

Joe carefully maintained his machines. He'd oil, grease, repair belts and fuel the tractor. One year he was pouring gas while the tractor was running; he slipped, and a large quantity of gas spilled on the hot engine and ignited it. The gas and flames followed up the belt to the separator. It took him several weeks to repair it all, so everyone was late that year. After that, he always shut down the machine before he poured gas.

Sometimes the wind would change and blow all the straw and dust straight back across the machine and the teams of men throwing bundles into the separator and sacking grain. If it became really unbearable, they'd bitch to Joe until he moved the machine around so the tractor faced into the wind. This entailed folding and unfastening the apron and conveyor, taking off the main drive belt to the tractor, turning the straw blower and augers, moving everything to the other side and then setting it up again. Joe always leveled the machine by digging wheels down into the dirt which also helped stabilize the thresher. If everyone helped, this took half an hour.

If the wind shifted direction again, there'd be a volley of swear words. Joe wouldn't relent and the men would have to suffer the dust and chaff for the rest of the day.

The granary had galvanized metal siding and sits to the right of the house in this photo. You can see the tower room roof sitting on top of the granary.

During very rainy seasons the shocks never seemed to dry. On sunny days we'd take forks and rip the shocks apart so the sun and wind could do their work and be threshed at the end of the day. If there was another rain on these shocks, it would be a disaster, since sprouted grain couldn't be sold and made poor animal feed.

As a small child, threshing was great entertainment. It was fascinating for an inquisitive young boy. We'd crawl on top of a thresher with all the shakers moving and the head spinning and listen to the change of sounds as each bundle passed through. We'd watch 10 or 15 belts spinning to power the fans and augers. We'd breathe in the beautiful smells of fresh wheat, barley or even oats as we rode in the grain wagons on top of the grain sacks. We'd crawl in the bins in the granary and bury ourselves in the grain.

I remember seeing one of the last steam engines go by our farm. It was huge, slow and noisy. They loved to blow their whistles, which were so loud they could be heard miles away and it scared the hell out of a small farm kid when first he or she heard one. I can't remember ever having a steam engine on our farm for threshing, although it seems one time we had one for sawing wood. Soon they would be replaced by the more versatile, gas-powered tractors.

During threshing, steam engines could be fueled with straw. This kept a man busy feeding the fire to keep the steam up. With no straw in winter when wood was cut, they burned wood. The huge back wheels were 7' or 8' high with small cleats and were never much good at pulling a thresher in loose dirt or sand. Joe's early tractor had long steel lugs like wedges used in lumbering and could make it up any hill road. Sometimes 2 or 3 men would hang on the upper side of the thresher so it wouldn't tip over as a few had done in the past.

Sometimes, when Dad heard the price was going up, he might plant a field of flax. The stalks were so tough it was very hard on the thresher and Joe hated threshing it. The seed was slippery and would run out of the smallest hole in a sack or a grain box that could hold other grains. As ever, the next year the price was down and Dad wouldn't raise it again.

One year we planted 16 acres of rye on "new" ground on the Sleepy Hollow hill above the house we rented to George Broze and his family. The rye didn't lodge much. It stood straight and tall and was about six feet high. The binder could only be raised to 16" or so and the bundles ended up 5' long, heavy and slippery to handle. Fun, fun, fun.

All this excitement and last, but not least, for a kid, was the delicious, wonderful food with two lunches (at 10 & 3) and one dinner (12 noon) every day. We bought fresh meat in Red Wing from Bracher's for all the dinners, usually three. Even if we finished in 2 ½ days, we always served dinner before the threshing crew went to the next farm. Roast beef, mashed potatoes, a couple different vegetables, pickles, coffee, bars and always pie.

The women always served hearty meals. As a child, I ate after the men until I could work with them. I would eat at our close neighbors, the Hawkinson's, too, because Jimmy Jenson would be visiting. He was my age and we played together and this was less than ½ mile away, an easy walk for a small child. There were always sandwiches, cookies or cake left for me and lemonade. We always had fresh bread with lots of butter, either ham or summer sausage and, sometimes, Bracher's sausage, which was softer, with lots of spices and not home-cured. Wow!

Willy and Bob hated the food at one farm. Their meals were bad with chicken or chunky pieces of poor meat and Spam sandwiches. Ick! Kolshorns lost their wife/mother early, so they hired two neighboring women to cook for the thresher crew, apparently with ok results.

With technical advances during the Depression, in the late 30s, Dad found a used vertical grain elevator through Johnny Quell and installed it in the granary. Willy and Bob dug a large 5' wide and 6' deep pit along the center of the side wall, then broke through the rock wall into the granary basement. They formed and cemented up the pit and extended it into the basement, forming that part with wood.

Then they built a tower room on the roof directly above the pit and installed the head gears and an electric elevator motor that was 1½ horsepower. They installed 6" galvanized pipes to all of the bins below. The elevator was a continuous fabric belt 12" wide. Steel cups, one foot apart, were riveted to the belt. The cups picked up the grain in the pit and carried it to the top of the building, dumped the grain and continued back down — upside down, of course.

This was a more efficient way of handling grain. There was no sacking or lifting or grain hauled loose. The elevator did the work of three men. Dad leveled the wagon by the thresher. Since we were one of the first to have an elevator, our neighbors were a little jealous and desired to prove one man (Bob) could not keep up with the machine and keep the grain away.

This reminds me of the night Marilyn and I spent in Cortona, Spain, which is about 28 miles from Seville. The Spanish have a similar but worse problem: too much grain trash that would not rot in their dry soil. So they burn it, so they can plant again. We stayed in an old restored castle high on a hill with stone walls 30" thick. At night we looked out of the windows across a plain of 50 miles or more and saw hundreds of fires burning all night with continuous thunder and wild heat lightning from a strong plains wind. It was one of the most awesome sights we'd ever seen and we stayed up for hours watching.

They threw the bundles into the separator as fast as the cylinder, grinding and howling, would take them. Normally, Joe would have stopped them from stressing the machine, but he joined the conspiracy. The threshers were working up on the hill. Bob didn't take time to chain the back wheels to help hold back the heavy load of grain as it went down the hill and the horses ran down the hill road at full speed.

He'd back into the pit, open the end gate and shovel out the wagon. He didn't even wait to shut the elevator off but got Gim to do that. He'd run the horses up the hill back to the rig just in time, much to the neighbors' disappointment, but they kept trying. About two in the afternoon, Dad could see this team of horses would not last the day. As Willy was unloading his bundles, they switched horses. Only once during the day did Joe shut down the machine for a few minutes. It was a small victory for the neighbors. The next day even the bundle haulers were tired and things slowed to a normal pace and we knew we had won!

Sometimes the thresher's shaft boxes would heat up and require repeated oiling. Sometimes belts broke. Joe kept several rolls of different width belt material handy and a box of end cleats and pins to make new belts. In the morning, the belts would be tight from the dew. As the day warmed, the belts stretched and required tightening or while the belt was running, the application of a tube of sticky stuff. The cylinder head was tightened or loosened depending on the type of grain. The dump bucket had to be changed for the weight of different types of grain. When we hauled loose grain, the dump bucket was disconnected and the grain continuously ran out.

To "settle up" threshing, on a Saturday night everyone got together, including the children! Each farmer kept a record of the number of hours threshed on his farm. If not, they could get the figures from

The threshing crew on the Joachim Deden farm. Can you imagine providing a noon meal for 20 hard-working members of a threshing crew that were at your farm for many days along with your normal family members?

Joe, who kept track of how many men and how many teams each farm contributed to his farm and compared this with what he had provided for use on other farms and for how long. If the Horns had only two men at your place for 2 ½ or 3 days and you had three men at Horn's for two days, the hours and teams were close. After this was all straightened out, not much money ever changed hands. I would guess probably $10 to $50. The big bill was for Joe, for his machine and gas. All of this was figured out with rarely an argument. You'd usually give a few dollars rather than have a falling out with our neighbors.

After "settling up" came the fun and the big night supper with Bracher's wieners and Bracher's pickled pigs feet, city buns, ham, pickles and all the beer you could drink. The beer came from Remler's brewery of Red Wing, either a quarter barrel or a number of cases of "picnics," in tall, brown glass bottles. The early ones had lead stoppers with a clamp down wire. They were two quarts each, 55 cents per bottle, four in a case. We always returned the empties! These were the cause of my first hangover, with many more to come! You can be as sure as hell that the next morning, of all Sundays, Mother insisted we go to church.

Beer or pop was never served anywhere during the Depression years. Even root beer was too precious to serve threshers and was saved as a family treat.

After threshing, the first task was to clean up around the straw piles and haul some to the farm buildings. Usually Dad needed a rest, so we rarely got to it till after a rain. The edges of the piles had sprouted and turned green, especially after the first year of loose hauling when the men stuffed the machine to challenge the efficiency of our elevator. That year, the sieves in the shaker couldn't handle the volume of material going through and some grain went out the blower. The challenge of cleaning up the straw pile was to get a sleigh close to the straw pile and fork the loose straw right into the wagon.

Later, Ed Deden bought a small machine with a rubber belt that wound the straw into round bales. The straw had to be pitched by hand into the machine. It stopped every time a bale was ejected. This still saved a lot of work because it was easier to handle and to store the bales under roofs. We were thankful when he brought his machine down and baled our straw.

Willy, Dad and I usually cleaned around the piles. If we had too much straw, we'd haul away small loads and burn it. It could have been plowed under for humus but that was impossible with a horse plow and there was downed grain, grass and weeds, all of which had to be plowed under.

My grandfather, William Hayman Jr., purchased a wine press from Joe Zignago's Italian grandfather and they made lots of wine. Marilyn and I used it to grind our apples into juice every year. As I turn the screw down on the press I can still hear Dad say, "Not too tight. You wanna break it?" And yes, Dad, I still oil the gears every time I use it. I wash it carefully and pick out all the apple pieces out of the crushing gear.

Nephew Joe Deden and grandson with the Hayman family cider press 2017. "As I turn the screw down on the press I can still hear Dad say, 'Not too tight. You wanna break it?'"

Dog Days of Summer

During fall, Bob had the job of "skim plowing" just 2" deep, on fields full of witchgrass with a sulky plow and five horses. Every day, he'd harness the horses, plow all day long, unharness the horses, curry them and put grease on sores around their necks. Every day. After skim plowing there were several spring toothings to loosen and uproot the quack grass roots so the sun could kill them. This soil preparation method worked partially in dry years and in wet years seemed to make invading grasses grow even better. Four horses had a constant job of pulling the spring tooth and the teeth were continually raised to let trash drop out. This worked best after a hard rain.

We'd fill the barn with second-cut hay and top off sections of the hay shed before threshing began in August. The third-cut hay in September was only alfalfa. It took 3 or 4 days to dry, as the sun was lower. It was excellent hay, green, tender and great-smelling. This hay was stored all around the calf barn, the hog house and any little corner to be found. Sometimes we put a load or two on top of the hay bins that had settled. If the temperature was cool, this was not a bad job.

Breaks between "big" jobs, like haying and threshing, were filled with hundreds of "little" jobs. We'd re-roof sheds, re-shingle the granary, build temporary fences in the meadow, quarry rock, haul gravel for the driveway, repair buildings, add onto sheds or old buildings, cut weeds, check the grain to be sure it did not heat.

> This reminded me of when Marilyn and I drove the old "Blue Highway" in central Nebraska. Every 10 miles we'd see a small town drying and processing alfalfa.

In the late summer and early fall, we'd pick chokecherries or crabapples for jelly. We'd gather walnuts, shell and wash them and collect butternuts to dry. We'd clean the main freshwater cistern on the hill or pull a well pump and replace the pipes or leathers.

This was the time of year we'd cut 4" to 12" oaks for fence posts and peel bark with an ax or draw shave. The larger posts were used for permanent fences and the smaller ones for temporary fences. All were piled off the ground to dry. Modern fence posts are chemically treated to retard rotting. Our oak fence posts would last 10 to 15 years. As they aged and became more rotten, the posts became great homes for bluebirds and red-headed woodpeckers.

Picnic at the Quells. Dora is sitting lower right with Adeline. Gim and baby Milt are next to them to their left. Edith is left of Milt.

We cut cottonwoods for saw logs for buildings, hay racks or other farm uses. We'd load and haul, 1-5 on a wagon. Large logs were pulled up a side hill and, using smaller posts, were rolled onto a wagon and then tied down with log chains. We hauled many loads to the Frontenac sawmill that was along a stream some 7 miles away. Weeks later, we picked up the sawed lumber, hauled it back home, stacked it with cross pieces and covered it with tin to dry for a year. We'd take five loads of logs down and haul two larger and heavier loads of lumber back home!

Hauling gravel for our drive was done with a heavy wagon with 6" loose planks that were laid side by side, flat on the bolsters and 8" side planks and ends. Dad searched the ditches for a vein of gravel. Then he'd drive the team into the ditch and we loaded it with hand shovels. He'd return to the driveway, take out the ends and one side and tip the gravel from each 6" plank and then go back for more.

Early sawmill. Note the sawyer sharpening the saw with a file as a dull saw would not cut straight. "We'd take five loads of logs down, haul two larger and heavier loads of lumber back home, stack it with cross pieces and cover it with tin to dry for a year!" Fillmore County Historical Society Photo.

"Breaks between 'big' jobs, like haying and threshing, were filled with hundreds of 'little' jobs. Hauling gravel for our drive was done with a heavy wagon with 6" loose planks that were laid side by side, flat on the bolsters and 8" side planks and ends."

Stone Foundations

Quarrying limestone rock was interesting, back-breaking work. The quarry was half-way up the Sleepy Hollow road. First we removed the overburden by shoveling it into a wagon then dumped it over the hillside. Sometimes the soil, loose rock and tree roots were two to 3' deep before we reached the first level of stone. The top rock layers could be easily broken apart with wedges and a maul. Often they had horizontal frost seams 4", 6", 8" to 10" deep where wedges could be driven in to loosen a seam. We'd force crowbars into the small cracks, raise the ledge and then slip a rock or piece of wood under its center. With a stone hammer, we'd break the rock into usable squares to use for building foundations.

This went well until we got to 12", 18" or 24" ledges without frost cracks. We'd drilled a hole where we thought the rock would break, filled it with black power and a fuse and blasted. Sometimes it broke right, other times, not at all. If all failed, we'd dig behind the ledge, find a hole, dig it out and pack in several sticks of dynamite and light the fuse. Rock was thrown all over the quarry and the road. Sometimes it would work, sometimes not. Or it would loosen a ledge enough for us to work it down. We'd break more stone and discard some of the angle pieces. When the area was filled with piles of workable stone, we'd load them on our wagon and haul them home where either they were stockpiled or, in the case of the new machine shed, dropped all around the new foundation for easier accessibility. Charley Sip liked the rock put right where he was to lay it. To build a straight wall, the rocks would need to be worked up further with a stone hammer.

Our machine shed was 40' x 80' with two central sliding doors. It was the result of Bob and Willy putting continuous pressure on Dad. They'd refuse to struggle fitting the two binders in the hayloft of the barn and annually having to pull it back out the next summer after all the corn fodder had been blown over them in the mow. Dad finally relented and started quarrying rock and sawing logs for roof boards and 2x6 studs and plates. Eventually the building was part home-sawn lumber and part timber from northern Minnesota.

In March 1936, Dad hired John Peters and his crew to build the machine shed. Peters was a German with an elf-like face. He had a mustache and wore small metal-rimmed glasses. He was a good carpenter and knew how to use a square. He rarely made an error. Old timers said if you knew how to use a square, you could build anything. We helped nail on roof boards where we couldn't do too much wrong. It was tough

The garage sits in the foreground of this photo and the shed is to the right of the hay shed.

for a youngster to nail the hard oak boards and resulted in lots of bent nails and sore thumbs.

The shed held all our limited machinery, except two hay wagons, the old dump rake and the tedder. These relics of the past were parked in the back behind the shed by the willows. The feed mill was moved over to the shed from the barn, with the pulley accessible through the big door opening, so it could be more easily attached to a tractor. We added a raised platform to more easily feed the mill.

Another major building project was a new, story and a half, two-car garage and workshop. Quarried rock was used for the footings and foundation. Dad found the City of Red Wing was tearing down the old Women's Seminary and a huge pile of bricks were available for nothing. The catch was two sides of the brick were covered with old cement. For months on end, it became my job to chip off the cement and pile the clean bricks.

The building was constructed of brick. The inside had plastered walls and the outside plaster was covered with stucco. The corner near the barnyard eventually was worn smooth, as the cows found it an agreeable place to scratch their hides. One side of the garage held the old re-built Studebaker truck and the other, the Dodge touring car, until Dad bought the 1941 Studebaker Champion.

The anvil and forge paraphernalia went into the shop, along with an old, long wooden bench with a wooden vise, new benches for a wood lathe, band saw, drill and a metal vise.

When these buildings were completed, the old mill was torn down. Ground feed was stored in the new machine shed or put into a grain box and hauled to the barn. The blacksmith shop was used to store old iron and our sleighs. The corn shredder found its off-season home in a lean-to against the open-ended, upper corn crib.

All summer, I mowed our lawn with an old reel-type push mower that was dull as hell. The house was on a steep hill and our lawn was huge. During August and September it was solid crabgrass! I helped Dad spray apple trees with an old pump sprayer tank set on one wheel. It didn't work very well and most years our apples were wormy. Dad would always say, "When I eats apples, worms, look out for yourselves." Dad recalled when he was growing up as a kid, going up into the hill orchard during spring thaws and eating soft mushy apples emerging out of the snow, just to get something sweet to eat.

"The house was on a steep hill and the lawn was challenging to mow with an old reel-type mower that was dull as hell."

Gofer Jobs

As the smallest, I was given the gofer jobs. I'd get to gofer this and gofer that. Carry or hold lanterns. Get pails. Shut off the water. Turn on the water. Close doors. Stand in a door and don't let "it" out. Feed the chickens. Pick up the eggs. Get a shovel. Get the crowbar. Get the post-hole digger. Get a flat wrench. Get a monkey wrench. Get a combination wrench.

Later, get the vise grip. Get the scoop shovel. Get the oil can. Get the axle grease. Get the cows. Get the horses. Chase the chickens out of the yard. Beat the rugs. Beat the mattress. Get the stock dip. Get the turpentine. Get a jug of water. Get the lunch. Get more water. Get the milk from the cistern. Hang the root beer in the cistern (one job I liked). Feed the dogs. Carry wood into the house. Feed the cats. Feed the calves in the yard. Re-stake a calf on the lawn. Turn the separator. Turn the grindstone. Turn the ice cream maker (2nd job I liked). Run down and fill the kerosene can. Fill the reservoir at the end of the stove with soft water from the cistern (women especially liked it for washing their hair).

Get the flyswatter. Get a bottle of beer from the basement. Get a jar of corn. Get a jar of beans. Get some potatoes. Get a head of cabbage. Throw a piece of wood on the furnace. Close the hill gate. Close the covers on the stock tank. Close the lower gate. Pick some crabapples. Run get me some onions. Get me some dill. Get a couple of cucumbers. Get that rug off the line. I need a hot fire to fry steak. Get me some kindling. Keep the cats away from the meat while I'm gone. Get me a butcher knife. Get the other ax. Watch the cows along the road. Give the cows ground feed. Feed the horses a bucket of oats. Dump this garbage in the compost pile. Run upstairs and close the windows before the storm. Run out and take the towels off the line, it's starting to rain. Run up and turn the windmill off. Get my hoe; I left it in the garden. Be a good boy and run up and get the mail. I need some parsley, be a good boy…be a good boy…be a good boy and get me…

"Be a good boy" carried a little sniveling condescension but not enough to countenance a refusal! I learned from Willy and Bob, and some days I'd just hide! And some days I'd go over to Aunty Broze and tell her my troubles. No one would listen at home and they all had more troubles than me! Sisters: newer dresses and ribbons. Brothers: money for a gun and shells. Me: a nickel for licorice at Hansen and Gustufson. Mom: a few quarters for the collection plate on Sunday so Reverend Bauman could eat well! Well, bless my soul! Dora was certainly dedicated to advancing God's interest here on earth, at least with herself and her daughters. Adeline accepted it as a means to an end, while Edith accepted religion only to a point, questioning some of its meanness.

Milt with pet fox that he had for three years.

Bozo, the Wonder Dog

In September, we cut our third crop of alfalfa. Once, Willie was on Sleepy Hollow hill when up came a pretty relative of the Broze girls from Minneapolis. She had one green eye and one brown eye and her body parts were well-placed and proportioned.

Willy said, "Would you like a ride on my side delivery rake? Would you like to share my lunch? Would you like to get alfalfa leaves in your hair and thistles in your bottom?" After three or four days, Gim saw the picture and told her to go home and stay there. For a while it did not make for pleasant interactions with our renters.

I often wondered why Bob and Willy never played around with Bunny and Elma Broze. They were both good-looking, slim, although flat-chested. Muggs was the heavy, less attractive one! No doubt Dad scared the hell out of 'em about the evils of girls and all their lovely things and how they could send a young man to Hell or the doctor.

The simple truth was, Bob and Willy were shy and never associated girls with pleasure. They thought them to be mysterious beings whose ways were far from those of hunting and baseball. Every girl with two legs and long hair triggered my brain into a torrent of erotic thoughts. That's probably why I was never a great hunter or liked baseball.

Muggs kept the family from freezing some winters by going into the wooded hills with a Swede saw or bow saw. She'd climb an oak tree, straddle a dead branch and saw it off in front of her. After she cut four or five limbs, she'd pull them down the hill to their house. There she'd put them on a saw horse and cut them into stove-sized pieces. In a day or two, she'd do the same thing. In the spring we saw the paths where she had pulled branches down the hill. In later years I'd walk those hills and see oaks with a 16" sawn-off stub where Muggs had done her work.

George Broze, her father, would help on our farm when he was out of work by quarrying rock, shocking corn and helping with other projects. In return, we would fork two loads of hay into his barn. It was enough to get his three cows through the winter. Dad occasionally would forget the rent and even give him a few dollars or some meat.

The Brozes had a big German shepherd dog named Bozo, a fairly friendly mutt, once people got past his bark and growl. In his younger years, Dad would walk by Broze's with his 22 Special and pick up Bozo to go hunting. Bozo was good at treeing partridge and Dad would shoot them. Everything was hunky-dory between Dad and Bozo until one spring they'd been cutting wood near the Broze home. Dad filled some logs with black powder and set them off, just when Bozo meandered over the ridge to see if any hunting was on deck. Well, he was close when the powder went off.

Something must have snapped in Bozo's brain. He took off 90 miles an hour towards home, where he headed for the outhouse and jumped down the toilet hole. Next morning, the first person visiting the outhouse became frightened by the strange noise rising from below. Rescuing him entailed tipping over the outhouse and crawling into the hole to help him out. Bozo was a different color over the lower portion of his frame. His rescuer came out looking and smelling just like Bozo.

Bozo was permanently impacted by the blast. A severe electrical storm would send him to the outhouse. George eventually put a hook on the door.

George Broze on left with Bozo.

Harvest Moon

Sometimes during the month of September we had quiet spots in the farm work, but October brought full work. For days on end, Bob and Willy worked on the corn binder with three horses. The binder cut the corn one row at a time. The corn stalks were 5' to 6' high and stood upright on the binder until an arm drew a string around them, tied a knot, cut the string and ejected the bundle onto a conveyor belt. When the belt was full, it was activated and it dumped the bundles in one spot. If the prison-made twine was uneven, it often broke and had to be retied by hand.

The damn knotter constantly malfunctioned. We'd adjust it, repair, readjust and swear! Unlike Rabelais' Friar John who said, "I only swear to embellish my language, it's rhetorical coloring," we swore to release tension. We couldn't kick our brothers or hit our Old Man when we smashed our knuckles against a raw-edged piece of machinery trying to get a rusty nut loose. It was a psychic release to swear. With playmates, the "F word" was, of course, "rhetorical coloring," of the lowest form, a word void of any thought. It was Donnie and Robbie's favorite! I tried the "F word" on Willy once and he said, "Don't you let Mom hear you say that. She'll wash your mouth out with soap!"

To shock corn bundles, one person held three bundles upright to form a tripod while another piled bundles around them. When it stood, the tripod holder would step back and help pile 10 to 12 more bundles to the shock. The real fun began as we'd stand on a stool and draw a string around the top of the shock, hug it with our arms, with our face right into the dry, sharp leaves and then slip one end of the string into the other looped end, draw up tight and tie a square knot. We were careful not to pull too tight or the string could break and we'd have to start all over again. This was hard, tiring work. The bundles were awkward and heavy and made our arms, neck and face sore and raw from the razor-like corn leaf edges.

For a young boy, then came endless hours after school of walking round, picking up corn ears with a single horse and stone boat. We went up and down the rows and snapped off missed ears of corn, especially on the ends where the stalks were knocked over turning round. By shoveling just half the load to the hogs, this chore could be reduced to an every other day job.

October was also the month for digging, picking up and hauling two acres of potatoes. It was a month of endless days hauling split wood, tossing it into the woodshed or carrying load after load of chunks into two furnace rooms. This left no time for playing with the neighbor boys.

We'd pick apples, all but the Greenings which were safe till November. When wild grapes were sweet, Dad would carry an

"To shock corn bundles, one person held three bundles upright to form a tripod while another person piled more bundles around them." Goodhue County Historical Society Photo.

extension ladder into the woods and gather them into a bucket. He'd let the bucket down with a rope and I'd dump the grapes into baskets. These were made into wine or grape juice, which was canned.

Late in October and into early November, day after day, we'd hitch up the five horses for deep plowing (5" to 6") the earlier, skim-plowed fields. Succumbing to Bob and Willy's pressure, around 1938 Dad tried a Minneapolis Moline tractor. Dealers would loan them out for several days, even a week. We'd plow like hell, then send it back saying we'd "think about it." Then we tried out a John Deere and an Oliver and after three tractors and 17 days, we had all our fall plowing done. We didn't buy anything until the following year, when Dad bought a medium-size Minneapolis Moline Z that had rubber tires.

Dad thought the new tractor would be good for stationary belt work but Bob talked him into putting it on our grain binder. Dad said, "Do you want to wear it out right away?" He was afraid the rubber tires would spin down into the ground, but they worked better than steel lugs. The Hawkinsons saw how well they worked and changed their wheels from lugs to rubber!

Some fields of corn were left standing to be husked by hand with a "husking peg." It was a metal hook strapped to your hand. We'd grab a cob, pull back the husk, snap the cob from the stalk and toss it against the "bang board." "Bang board?" We'd work fast, taking just a few seconds taking no time to aim. With our head always down, we'd throw the cob against a large board standing up at the far side of the wagon. "Bang!" It bounced off the board into the wagon. When the box was filled, we drove the team alongside the corn cribs and shoveled the ears of corn in.

Sometimes winter caught up with us before we finished husking. Dad would say, "The partridge will eat our corn in the field this year." In spring, husking would resume as soon as the snow was gone and the ground was still frozen, as the fields had to be cleared for plowing.

Down in Iowa they had husking bees with prizes given for the most corn husked in a specific period of time. Winners were written up in local papers and progressed on to national contests.

By early November the corn shredder was pulled up to the barn. It was leveled, greased, the belt attached, the blower pipe stuck into a hole under the roof, the tractor set up and the belt was attached to the shredder. Thus we began a 2- to 3-week late fall job. Corn bundles were laid on a platform next to the roller head. A knife to cut the twine was tied to the platform with a string, so it was always at hand. The long bundles were fed into the snapping rollers head first. The leaves, husks and stalks were crushed and blown into the barn for fodder. It covered most of the mowed hay as well as the binders and

Corn "leaves, husks and stalks were crushed and blown into the barn for fodder."

other machinery stored there.

Cows ate the corn husks and leaves but left the stalks. They were thrown into the steer pens to soak up you-know-what. Digging manure out of the pens was very difficult because of the length of the stalks and their compaction by hooves.

Corn ears were augered out the back of the shredder into a grain box. They usually were only half-husked so this was a rather inefficient machine. Ears for cattle feed had to be further husked by hand or they would plug the feed mill. The hogs readily husked their share.

Many times we were caught in the first snows or ice storms that froze the bundles to the ground. The barn was built at the base of a hill. The work area had a steep incline leading to the second level of the barn. Oftentimes, we shredded corn into December enduring mud, rain, snow, sleet, cold spells and breakdowns, not to mention colds and illnesses. With daily chores in between, our heavy winter routine started. When the snow got too deep, we'd switch from wagon wheels to sleighs. Eventually we built a third corn crib. When the new machine shed was built, the feed mill was moved there. We'd dump a large pile of corn inside, near the mill, so it was handy for grinding.

Corn harvesting tools. A corn husker's glove called a husking peg was used to remove corn husks from the cobs. The metal teeth were used to remove corn kernels from the cob, with the same one being used for popcorn. Charles used this sheller and ground corn kernels to make johnny cake or corn bread.

During a winter storm, it was always a problem to get the last young livestock into the barn. They had become wild over the summer and were not comfortable around humans. They combatively turned on our dogs and gave them trouble attempting to help move the critters into the barn. The pigs were more compliant and went in on their own. The horses, too, were glad to get out of bad weather!

During the winter, we constantly had to clean the barns and pens. We used the manure spreader until the snow was 8-12" deep and the wheels wouldn't turn. Then we'd use the sleigh to spread the manure with muscle power and return to the barn with a load of straw. The daily routine was to load the manure out and put clean straw in. Feed, water, and clean. A continuous round of recycling hay and grain through animals and then out onto the fields for next year's fertilizer.

Farming was a labor-intensive business. It was often very stressful and weather dependent. Even if you wanted to get ahead and worked very hard, you often ended up only eking out a minimal level of existence.

Depression and suicides were not infrequent among farmers during those years. Banks foreclosed on farms for as little as $250! The banks never wanted the principal back, just the interest. Many farmers couldn't even pay that, and too many lost their farms. This created a great distrust of banks for 20 or 30 years thereafter. This sordid history is recorded in the farms' Abstracts throughout the Midwest.

By late fall many jobs were finished. We winterized the stock tank, piled straw on water connections that might freeze and maybe butchered an early hog for December and holiday meals. We moved the cream separator from the unheated back kitchen into the house until April and shut off all outside water faucets. If it was a snow-free fall, we'd start cutting wood. On stormy afternoons or evenings Willy would crack walnuts and butternuts for Christmas candy and cookies.

The Universal Tinkerer

Before my time, it was decided the boys would go to the Episcopal church and the girls would attend the German Lutheran church. This situation created hundreds of Sunday morning battles between my parents.

> "Charles, aren't you going to take the boys to church?"
> "Can't you leave a poor body rest?"
> "If they were Lutherans, they'd be in church! Don't you ever consider their souls? How will they get to Heaven?"
> "You do enough praying for everyone." On and on…

Some Sundays this exchange lasted for hours, with both parties staying angry all day.

As a small child I went to the Lutheran church with Mom because I hoped to get a piece of licorice downtown after the service. What a price to pay for sitting an hour or more under Rev. Bauman's Hell and Brimstone. When we left church some old gals would come up to Mom and say, "And this is 'the Baby' of the family?" This really pissed me off to no end. Imagine being called a baby at the age of 10! I had to continually restrain myself from kicking them in the ankles, but then I wouldn't get any licorice. I was a victim of my addiction!

The 1867 photo of the Moser family shows Sarah Moser, 2nd from the left, who was William Hayman Jr.'s first wife. Note: a Bible is prominently displayed on the table.

About age 12, I was told I was not to be saved by Rev. Bauman's crowd, that the Episcopalians had the proprietary rights to protect me from Hell and turn me toward the right path. It was quite a shock, but at least the licorice kept coming.

I was 14 when I had to take eight weeks of instructions to get confirmed. It turned out okay because a number of the kids were in my high school classes. Also, we had an early Sunday morning breakfast which consisted of orange juice and sweet caramel rolls. Rev. Moe was laid back. "You guys look like you were over at Bay City (bar) too long last night." Another plus: Janet Nelson, a well-endowed blonde from my class, was learning the same doctrine!

I usually hated going to church. Dad would come in late and sit up front and fall asleep. He'd bob his head, or worse, rock back and forth when the congregation was singing a hymn he liked. Midnight

In *An Instance of the Fingerpost*, Ian Pears described, "The mean piety, the self-importance of these people (Puritans) their insufferable reproaches and pained kindnesses…" We still have them—beware of the "dry"—too religious a person! Samuel Butler described them: "too religious to consider Fortune a deity at all!"

"Serve your fellow man." Hell, send him out into the desert and maybe he can become a demigod and serve! Or, as they say, (that wonderful group of "they": how many million nibbles of philosophy have "they" espoused), "Church is ok for them that needs it." Too much dogma, too little Art.

1925 photo of Grandpa William Hayman Jr, with Bob, Wilbur, Adeline and Edith.

Services on Christmas Eve were tolerable because the whole church was lit with candles in the windows and green pines decorated the altar. The choir was exceptionally good and I enjoyed Christmas carols. If only Dad's head didn't rock so much!

I had another problem. Every time I stared at Janet Nelson, the blood started to surge around my body. Both my mind and body were in a cooperative state of sin, even as Christ looked down at me from the altar. He was dead and Janet was very much alive! I hoped my mother who was a block up the street in her brick edifice could not read my "sinful" thoughts.

Around this time, E. H. Foot, owner of the R.W. Tannery gave the huge sum of $30,000 for a new organ that was considered the finest of its type. Certainly it was loud, and loud is good in an Episcopal church.

It was at the end of my senior year when Janet and I were in a contest to see who could memorize and recite the most lines of poetry to Signe Anderson for extra credit in our English class. We were neck-and-neck when she recited some more the last week of school and taunted me with it. I memorized some more and came back the next day but Signe said Janet had won. I never saw Janet until 30 years later at a class reunion and did not recognize her! Nature had been hard at work destroying the beauty of that pretty peony blossom.

That summer, my interest turned to Joanne Wintervold. She was an attractive sloe-eyed blonde whose daddy was a banker. She lived up on the edge of the bluff.

Religion was divisive and caused constant fights and broken love affairs which could have worked out beautifully for my siblings, if not for distrust and hatred of other dogmas. If there is a God, I'm sure this is not what He or She intended!

The truth is, I was never much of a Sabbatarian. The most I could cotton to was a modest reduction of my Sunday toils in respect to the great Universal Tinkerer! I never thought my fellow man trained in dogma and physical greed had a better handle on interpreting life's road to pleasure and the unknowable "Hereafter."

If there is a God, He or She must be an understanding one and not fault any questioning, wondering or even doubting. Certainly not a vengeful being (male, female, or genderless), or whatever other form, shape, composition, or spirit it may be.

Don't know. So many wonders—beautiful—natural—and Man: There must be a Creator! But…so many horribly bad things. Maybe the earth is an anomaly, an accident, a gaseous, amoebic wonder? Maybe!

My mother knew there's a God and you better damn well believe and obey Him or you're going straight to Hell!

Oscar Hawkinson always said, "There's Santa Claus to scare kids and Christ to scare adults."

The Lutheran church was a rectangular box. In and out, the Episcopal church had a beautiful design. It had a high-pitched roof, two rows of wood columns down each side and beautiful windows. I would sit and admire the amazing stained glass. In Mom's Lutheran church, I counted the squares on the altar ceiling, or the pipes of the organ. You didn't get to me, Rev. Bauman. Ha! Ha! "Reverend Picksniff."

The pressures of farm work often came before the duty to attend church, especially in fall. Our cousin Henry's son died one fall. The church was packed and the preacher had a large, captive audience to be excoriated for hours. The devout assembly nervously watched a gathering snow storm with falling temperatures and heavy winds. They knew their horses and stock were exposed and needed immediate care. The good preacher was oblivious to their concerns and droned on until he felt they'd been sufficiently chastised.

When Mom was buried, the Lutheran preacher said, "Here lies a sinner." When the priest buried Loretta Sip, he said, "Here lies a charitable woman." We all agreed if there was anyone in the world who was not a sinner, it was Mom.

One last joke related to religion that came from Horace Greeley's newspaper. Question: When is the best time to cut elders? Answer: Just before camp meeting! Which reminds us of several famous paintings relating the story of Susannah and the Elders—the lascivious old men watching the young beauty at her bath.

Attending Sara Golisch and Loren Heintz's wedding on June 4th 1988 are left to right: Fran and Wilbur Hayman, Janet Hayman Golisch, Milt and Marilyn Hayman, Adeline Hayman Deden and Vince Deden.

Get Togethers

Our social life with neighbors was usually focused around the exchange of labor. The men sawed wood, threshed, butchered and erected buildings together. Before my time there was an adult card club with folks not more than a mile away: the Jensons, Millers, Schillings, Dedens, Grosses and Kohrs. That ended with the Depression.

Some summer evenings, Oscar Hawkinson would walk up the valley to our house with two cigars. He'd sit in the big rocking chair on our porch and smoke and talk politics, mostly about Roosevelt and his Administration, the WPA (Works Progress Administration), CCCs (Civilian Conservation Corp) and the weight of the Depression. Dad was a dyed-in-the-wool Democrat and Oscar was a Republican. No voices were raised except when George Broze came over to pay the rent. He'd been an amateur boxer in his youth and he'd spent some time in the Red Wing Training School, a juvenile detention facility. He was a wild-eyed Democrat. He loved his beer, and would often get into bar fights if anyone said anything against Franklin Delano Roosevelt.

Later, during WWII, he was a self-appointed seeker-outer of pro-German sympathizers, especially around Floyd's Tavern. "Those __ __ Hitler lovers!" I believe there were many German sympathizers in our area who said little. Then, later in the war, when Gold Stars started to show up in windows, many of these sympathizers altered their attitudes.

Our own grandmother "Gim" came from Germany at age 8. She told how when living there, she would go down to the river and collect eels that had been thrown out by the fishermen. I guess they ate them. She also told about her bad trip over on the boat which was cold and wet, with only stale bread and lard to eat. Gim recalled the long voyage and their arrival at Ellis Island where she clung to her mother as they were herded like cattle. After the war, she sent care packages of woolen clothing to the Furstes, our relatives still living in Germany.

Gim's brother John was the first to leave Germany to avoid being drafted into the Prussian army. He wrote to his family and a year later they all came to the United States. They settled on a farm in Florence Township, south/southwest of Red Wing about 5 miles from our homestead. John later went to California.

Dad would often poke fun at the "Kraut eaters," low Germans, as unread or uneducated, having never read a book. In their defense, he considered they had well-kept, beautiful farms. After WWI, they had saved enough money selling wheat at $4.50 a bushel to buy farms for their sons at a price of $7,000 to $9,000 each. They built large well-maintained hip roof barns and had beautifully matched teams of horses. Our horse situation always upset Gim. She'd say we had, "A dog from every town," and none would ever be in step with its teammates. Our horses had one thing in common: they all loved oats.

Grandmother "Gim" came from Germany at age 8 (1878) and lived to be 86. She died in 1956.

During the Depression, unmarried women were referred to as old maids, such as Kate Miller and Mary Bartels. They worked doing cooking and household chores for room and board and a few dollars. "Friends" would come and stay, bringing along quasi-friends—in other words, free-loaders. One summer Mrs. Olson came out from Red Wing with friends from California. They were well-fed with generous farm meals for a few days and were "settling in" when Gim got a great idea. She made a huge pot of navy beans. She served beans for lunch, beans for dinner and after three days, they left. Nothing like beans and shoulder pork to get rid of tiresome guests!

Mom's sister, Martha Wittmeyer, would come and stay a week or more with her daughter Madeline. Martha had an air of saintliness. Boccaccio said it best when he described someone as so cold, butter wouldn't melt in her mouth. Years later, Bob and Willy laughed, remembering how Martha prayed before eating her oatmeal breakfast. She sat straight as a ramrod and pious as a Catholic saint. Never a smile or a funny word. She treated her sister with that "holier-than-thou" condescension. According to Martha, Mom had married a Yankee, and you know what they're like! "Yankee" was a term of derision used to refer to anyone who had roots in the North.

Martha was so saintly it was said the sheets of her conjugal couch were starched. Nothing soft or feminine in her personality, Martha was a truly religiously-minded woman of the time, who set about to do God's work to quell sin wherever she encountered its dark shadow.

Cousin Madeline and my sisters got along well together. She had a cat at home. Sometimes, I dried catnip, mailed it to her and she'd send me a quarter when she had money. She was our only 'ejeecated' cousin who never married, had a PhD and was a school principal. She was good looking. I suppose her pious mother had influenced her beyond help or at least beyond the idea of ever sleeping with a man and, as Rabelais expressed it, grinding their bacons together.

Adeline and Edith wearing buckle boots.

The Egg Pail and the Aunts
by Sister Janet Hayman Golisch as retold by her daughter, Sara Heintz.

Grandma Hayman's sisters were a bit judgmental of her circumstances on the Hay Creek farm. Their sheds were in poor shape, their chickens were scrawny, their horses didn't match, etc. So during one visit, Milt went out to gather the daily eggs and half filled the bottom of the pail with straw first. Then, he put the eggs on top until it filled the pail. He brought the pail into the house and gave it to Mom in the presence of the aunts so they could see what was gathered. They asked, "Did you get all those eggs today?" Of course Milt could honestly answer yes. "All those eggs were from those scrawny chickens!" They were impressed, and only Dora and Milt knew the truth. He liked to say his mom's eyes beamed in appreciation of his little trick. He felt a special connection to his mom that day. And the aunts weren't quite so critical of their farm.

In 1947, Dad and Mom built a new home where our neighbors, the Brozes, had lived. Willy and Francis Johnson were married and moved into our old farm home. Madeline was still freeloading on "Aunt Dora," and Mom called to bring her over to Willy's. That summer, I was working for Willy and intercepted this news and went to bed without telling anyone. Our time together got off to a bad start when Willy said, "Hello, Madeline." She bristled, gave him a cold look and responded, "My name is MAGDALENE." Willie never forgave her and never saw her in his home again.

A young Dora and Charles.

She asked if I went to bed immediately after Mom had called. Then Merlin, one of my neighborhood friends, called and I dressed and tore out of the house without so much as a "Hello." I was not one to bow down at the holy altar of Magdalene's education and piety. The following year, she rode out to California with Mom, who was poorer, but Magdalene never paid a cent for food or gas. So much for Christian virtue and stingy rellies. If ever they did something for my mother (which I doubt), it was little enough. "Works of charity faintly and coldly done lose their merit and signify nothing," Cervantes.

In the fall, Grant Puckards would come to the farm from the Cities with his family to hunt and have dinner and enjoy a leisure supper. His wife was a splashy blonde and a "hugger." I always had this thing about blondes.

The Puckards always brought something either candy or fresh fruit.

One time they brought a whole bag of 3M tape. The 3M company was still perfecting it and the cellophane tape would tear because the glue was stronger than the tape. They had just started manufacturing white Christmas tape with colored poinsettias on it. That Christmas, and for three or four more Christmases, every package was taped to the nines with it.

Mom cooked them good meals because they were not cheap with their presents. Willy had just bought his first scope for his 22 caliber rifle and had it well sighted-in. The three of us hunted all afternoon and traveled 6 miles or more. Willy dropped big fox squirrels from the very top of big oaks trees all shot in the head. We came home with 32 squirrels, which took an hour or more to skin and dress. Grant took them all and they went home happy.

One summer, Bill Peters worked for Dad. He and his brother Hank were brothers to Gim and Uncle William. Hank had a farm up in "Deutchland" and spoke broken English. As a small boy there were many families that spoke German in their homes. Their kids came to school speaking some English with a German accent. Hank had a Model T Ford and let Bob and Willy sit in the driver's seat and work the levers. Dad was going to kick them out, but Hank said, "No, Charlie, dey can't 'urt anyting."

Hank had an accident with his Model T Ford. At the trial the lady said he didn't signal when he turned. He told the judge, "If she could not see my car, 'ow would she ever see my 'and?"

She told the judge she smelled alcohol on him. He said, "Yes, Judge, I 'ad a sore shoulder from pitchin 'ay and I rubbed it down with rubbing alcohol." 'e won!

We exchanged dinners with several Red Wing families. We visited the Hoffmans. Mr. Hoffman lost a leg in WWI. We also saw the Sheraffs. He was a well-driller. They had a daughter, Gretchen, who was very pleasant and worked at the Ribbon and Fabric counter in the Dime Store. She always smiled and called, "Hello, Milty!" While sitting in Dora's church, I prayed she'd be transferred to the candy counter and give me 25 cents worth of candy for a dime. She always gave my mother and sisters extra yardage of ribbon, lace or fabric! I'm sure she has a preferred spot in Heaven that's ornamented with red and pink ribbons and fine Irish lace!

We'd share meals with one neighbor, Bill Miller and his wife Emma and their daughter "Little Emma". They moved from their hill farm down the valley three miles to the edge of Wells Creek. I always liked to go there because I could fish and swim in the creek. At our house, after the last bite of dessert, Mrs. Miller always got up and said, "Well, we'll have to do like the beggars do—eat and run." Later we often quoted her after an Easter or Thanksgiving Day dinner! The reason for the quick departure was evening chores needed attending at home.

Charles Hayman with cousin Bill Peters.

In our area, Goodhue County was made up of families of German and Scandinavian descent with a fair contingent of Irish in the west and southwest, and beyond that, tiny pockets of other nationalities. For the most part, the Germans never worked together or exchanged much labor with the Swedes or the Norwegians and there was no social intercourse among the families.

The Scandinavians considered Germans to be doltish, slaves to their farms and animals. They had no understanding of German humor and ethnic values and considered their ministers to be tyrants and oppressive. The Germans, on the other hand, thought the Swedes were lazy and very poor farmers. The Norwegians were considered strange, picky, prone to fights and not much better farmers than the Swedes. The Germans didn't understand their humor or ethnic ways and resented the Norwegians' interest in cultural things like reading and educating their children.

The two groups never trusted each other. They'd poke fun at one another and imitate their accents, ridicule their food and their ethnic backgrounds. "Krauts," "Dutchy," "Smelly Lutefisk." A big laugh was had over the dogs stopping to piss on the frozen lutefisk outside of Hanson and Gustafsons. Rumors had it that Swedish women were inclined to be promiscuous. The Germans were unresponsive, overweight baby factories!

This mostly died out with the change from agrarian to urban life. Although Dad warned Wilbur about marrying a Swede, saying

Visiting the Quells. In the 1930s and '40s, the Hayman family never owned a truck Left to right: Adeline and cousin Laura Quell sitting on the truck cab, Kate (last name unknown), Edith with one foot on the side board, Margaret Von Bargen, Mrs. Herman Peters, Gim is holding Milt, Margaret Quell (Gim's sister) and Dora.

they're "Not good housekeepers." But that was disproved when Willy married Fran. German Catholics stayed in their pockets and German Lutherans in theirs and they seldom mixed. Slowly, however, intermarriage broke these barriers, but not without many hardships. Inter-racial marriages sped up this evolution.

Our social life was an exchange of dinners, mostly with Mom's nieces and nephews on the Peters side. They all were good cooks, so the meals were always well-prepared and tasty. Sometimes, a little wine was served, but mostly we drank coffee and lemonade.

Mom's mother, Dorathea Rebecca Issendorf, died a few days after Mom was born. Mom was raised by her married sister, Maggie (Mrs. Wm. Peters), who lived on a farm in West Florence. It was there she lived and worked, and was raised with Maggie's children, her nieces and nephews, Adolph, Henry, Alfred, Emory and daughters Edna (who married a Hadler) and Wilhelmina (who married a Pagel) and Emma (who married a Breuer).

William Sr. was hired to make a cane that had a concealed knife in the end similar to a murder weapon. It was used as evidence in a trial. In the early 1850s he ordered a hand-made, combination rifle/shotgun with a hair trigger and silver inlays.

At dinners, I played with their children, who were my cousins. There was Merlin Hadler, Duane Pagel, Ralph and Russell Breuer, all children of Aunt Maggie's daughters and Marlin (Henry's son), Harold and Marvin (Alfred's boys) and some smaller Peters. We were all about the same age and played ball games together. The men played cards or sometimes horseshoes while the women worked and gossiped and they usually ate last.

Ralph and Russell wore size 13 shoes. Ralph married a tall redhead. They had a mega-son, Randy, who went on to achieve some pro basketball fame. We had dinner with Frank Leighten and his wife Barbara in London one summer. Frank was the retired coach of the Salt Lake City Jazz pro basketball team. I asked him if he knew Randy Breuer and he said he knew him very well. "A fine boy. He'd be making real money now, if he was still playing."

Mother had four sisters, Maggie (Peters), Lena (Reinke) and Emma (Lange), as well as Martha (Whitmeyer) and three brothers. Henry Jr. moved to Dumont MN; John acquired a good deal of farmland in North Dakota; Clarence moved to California.

Maria Peters (grandmother, "Gim"), Dad's mother, had four brothers: Herman, John, Hank and William; and a sister, Margaret, who became Mrs. Quell. Mom's rellies were good German Lutherans. Bob tells of Mission Fests Mom made him and Willie sit through that lasted 3 or 4 hours or all day. They sat on wood stools or on the ground and listened to the Hell and Brimstone preachers who came from all around. Bob said the best part was drinking the Green River pop that cost 5 cents a bottle.

We exchanged dinners with a few of Dad's relatives, especially the Quells who had two sons, Herman and Johnny. The meals were good at both places, but Johnny had geese and they would hiss and chase me. A stick was little defense for a small boy against any angry goose. Johnny did welding, brazing (cast iron) and repaired cars and machinery in his small machine shop. I'd often ride along with Dad to Uncle Johnny's when we had a piece of machinery that needed welding.

The great fun of the ride was to stop at the last of the country general stores in Belvedere Mills. At one time it had a pond and flour mill on Wells Creek. The store still had a few wooden barrels on the floor, tins of crackers, women's dresses and hats and old, black, high-button shoes that were out of style and unable to be sold. They had hundreds of utensils from the era of horse farming: buckets, pails, tubs, woolen cloth, racks, mattress beaters, fabric, flour and sugar in 100# sacks, men's workwear and old high black bowler hats.

The store went out of business when I was about 10 or 12. That auction had some items so old people didn't know what they were used for and sold for a few cents. Great antiques, unused!

My great grandfather, William Hayman Sr., was indentured for five years and apprenticed as a cabinetmaker in England. William had a very good friend who was a detective investigating a murder in London. He asked William to make a cane with a knife concealed in the end, similar to the murder weapon, to be used as evidence in the trial. The invisible knife was released by a brisk flip of the cane. When he learned William was going to America, he returned the cane noting that he might need it to protect himself. The cane has been one of my most interesting mementos.

The early nineteenth century was a period of widespread unrest. Europe was in revolt. Nationalism grew and the middle class began to openly oppose the aristocracy. Prussia was preparing for war. In 1848, a series of revolutions swept the continent. In England, Lord Raglan managed to control the mobs and avoid a similar uprising, but resentments ran deep.

William Hayman Sr. shared the bitterness against the aristocracy. In 1849, he left England with his wife and two children, 9-year-old William Jr., (my grandfather) and his sister Sophie, who was 3 or 4. The revolutions gave this country immigrants who were small business owners, and they possessed a variety of useful skills. The Haymans settled in Pennsylvania and remained there for six years. At that time, there was little call for fine cabinetry because the rich ordered what they wanted from Europe. My great-grandfather went to work for the Lakawanna Railroad as a pattern-maker and made wood patterns for steel castings.

It isn't clear why he chose to move to Minnesota. Before he left, he ordered a hand-made, combination rifle/shotgun with a hair trigger and silver inlays. This gun was left to me by my father, Charles. The gun cost $40. With wages of $1 a day, it took one year of savings. They traveled down the Ohio and up the Mississippi and landed at Frontenac, Minnesota, in 1855. The first task was to build a cabin of log and sod. He hired someone with a team of oxen to plow a small section of ground for crops and later bought his own team for $100.

"The store still had a few wooden barrels on the floor, tins of crackers, women's dresses and hats and old, black, high-button shoes that were out of style and unable to be sold." Minnesota Historical Society Photo.

Inventive Ways to Have Fun

Our entertainment was built around nature: forts, caves, hunting and hiking. Dad made everyone wooden skis. He worked down birch lumber thinner on each end and put a groove in the center. He then soaked the tips in hot water for several days and built a special rig to bend up the tips. This was put on top of the furnace for 4 or 5 days and the process was repeated until the tips had a nice gentle curve. He attached straps of leather about 1¼" wide to receive overshoes that were screwed on. Later he refined it by cutting ¾" rubber strips out of an old inner tube, which slipped over the toe and behind the heel and held the foot tightly in the strap.

Bob, Wilbur, Edith and Adeline dressed for outdoor winter fun!

The boys skied straight down the 300-foot sand hill slope at the schoolhouse and shot across the valley almost to Hawkinson's. The track was fast, icy and the hill was full of rocks. Willy was the best of the school kids, being either fearless or crazy. One time, Willy and I went out on the sand hill point. A large drift had formed on the top and he went 12' off the drift and down the hill. Remember the equipment he was using. I walked below the drift and started but fell twice before hitting bottom.

Most of the kids I went to school with were too timid to be skiers. Donnie and Robbie Sip didn't have skis. I skied with my sisters a few times but they were not crazy about the sport. Most favored sliding on a sled that had steel runners. We'd start below the hill cistern, go over the back kitchen bank, curve around the front of the house, turning and dragging the left foot, down the front hill, out the gate and across the drive. Sometimes we raised the lower barbed wire on the fence and had to duck low enough to shoot under the fence and into the cow yard. There were times I had to pick my stocking cap off a barb on my return.

My brothers and I would shovel out snow caves in a large drift. We'd crawl in, sit and tell adventure stories. Sometimes I brought a cat in with me but they never trusted me. In dry summers the cats would jump up on the cement cow tank and bend down 4-5" to drink. We'd sneak up behind them and tip them into the water! They'd give you that "I hate you," look, shake and crawl under a lilac bush to dry off.

Bob remembered that—before cars—they'd saddle a horse, tie a rope to the saddle and pull a skier. Bob used Pete, our white horse, who was fast. Joe Feldman had a little mare that left Pete in the snow crystals. Howard and Normie Hawkinson were also part of this snow sport.

Right after a winter storm, the most daring and exciting winter sport was before the roads were plowed. Bob or Willy would take the car, tie two 50' long ropes on the bumper and we'd ski behind. We'd go off the road way out into fields, over drifts, occasionally reaching speeds of 45 to 50 MPH. Considering our equipment, this was quite dangerous. Sometimes we'd flip the rope over the top of a mailbox or even a road sign. When a length of guardrail came up, a bridge or a large ditch that was not blown shut with snow, we'd have to quickly return to the road. Timing was everything and you got razzed if you dropped your rope, not making it to the road on time. Taking a spill at 30 or 40 MPH was a great challenge and dangerous! If we got way out on our rope, we could skid the rear of the car. The driver had to be prepared for this to happen. Adeline got quite good at this sport.

March brought melting snow and water freezing into ponds in the meadow. We'd skate on old, single-blade, clamp-on skates. We'd use a key to tighten the clamps on our work shoes or boots. Sometimes I'd take my sled, run like hell to the edge of the ice and belly-flop onto it. It was great fun but a nasty body bruiser! Later I bought a pair of size 12 hockey skates and filled the toes with newspaper, although it didn't make for proficient skating. A number of springs, we took wood and kerosene out to light a big bonfire along the ice with neighbor friends and, later, boyfriends and girlfriends.

My sophomore year in high school, I brought Punky North, my girlfriend at the time, out to skate. We took the pickup and spun around on the ice down by Hawkinson's so Dad couldn't see! I left my skates on to drive Punky back to Red Wing, which created some danger and a lot of hilarity.

Winter was the time to take aim with snowballs at the cows, calves and hogs. Our bull, Isaacbran (Big Business) was a prime target. You never wanted to irritate horses, because they'd get even. With humans, you had to pick your targets carefully or you'd get your face washed with snow if you couldn't outrun or out-climb your target. If I managed that, I'd stay away from them until they cooled down.

Home-made ice cream was a favorite winter treat. Mom would fill the large, cast iron cooking kettle in the cook shanty one-third full with water and then let it freeze. She'd start a fire, warm up the kettle to tip out the ice. Then she'd break the ice up with an ax, put pieces into a gunny sack and smash ice with the flat side of an ax. The process was repeated until the ice was fairly fine. Then it was put in a hand-cranked ice cream maker with coarse, unrefined animal salt to make the water super cold.

There was an inch and a half of space between the center one-gallon ice container and the outside wooden container. The inner container had center fins and two blades that rotated when we turned the crank. The container also rotated. We turned the crank and kept adding salt and ice around the container until we couldn't turn it any more. This could take an hour or more. Then we took out the center fins and blades and always argued over who would get to lick what. Care was taken because the fins were super cold and a tongue could stick to it, especially if it sat outside until supper, or if it was below zero on the back porch.

It was the richest, most delightful ice cream ever eaten. It was delicious food for the gods. It was a boiled recipe, made with 6 eggs, a quart of milk, two quarts of heavy cream, sugar, and lots of vanilla! Usually, we ate the whole gallon. If Willy made it or if he dished it out, he would pile his own dish 6" high. Sometimes we had it with angel food cake for February and March birthdays.

Returning from the fields in January with a load of straw or an empty manure wagon was fun because the horses were cold and wanted to get back to the barn and hay. They would run full-tilt with the sleigh sliding around corners. Willy would just let them fly and did not rein them in.

Animals had a salt lick outside, in summer, but in winter they got small amounts of salt sprinkled on their fodder.

One day Mom looked out the window, up to the second floor bedroom and saw yellow icicles hanging on the sill. She suggested that, in the future, Willy and Bob should come down stairs and go outside and use the outhouse!

When snow began melting, we'd spend hours redirecting or straightening streams of water running off the hills or making a snow dam to create a small lake behind it. The next day we'd break the ice or follow the swollen ditches full of snow from the spring melt cross-flooded fields, again breaking ice, or run and slide on it with our overshoes, sometimes venturing onto a snow bank along a flooded ditch and fall in up to our waists.

In April, I'd rake the lawn with my sisters. I'd haul away the dead grass in a wheelbarrow. We kept a constant fire burning to poke with a stick or maybe to roast marshmallows.

Easter time was exciting when I was a youngin. I'd fill a cardboard box with dead grass for a rabbit to lay eggs. I made other little grass piles around the yard, hoping this would produce more results from the Easter bunny. Even during the Depression the rabbit left me a large, hollow chocolate rabbit, several small, chicken-sized chocolate eggs with creamy maple nut inside and a liberal handful of jelly beans scattered in a reused basket.

Lucille Broze with Bozo the dog.

For several years I convinced Aunty Broze to let me put a rabbit box at her place. After cleaning up the loot in our yard, I'd run the half mile through the woods and across the valley. One year about sunup, I entered their yard and discovered my rabbit box was tipped upside-down. I ran into the house without knocking, (doors were never locked back then) and charged into George and Lucille's bedroom, interrupting some unfinished business. I shouted at the top of my voice, "I caught the Easter Bunny! I caught the Easter Bunny!" Well, the truth was the wind had come up over night and tipped it over. George and Lucille had partied late, fell into bed and were sound asleep. The last thing on their minds was a four-year-old looking for Easter eggs at 6 AM! One diverted my attention while the other snuck out and put some sweets under the box. I hope they forgave me for that intrusion!

I would go over to Aunty Broze and tell her my troubles. I'd complain about how hard they worked me, and she'd give me a handful of raisins or make me a fizzy drink which was cold water and lemon with a teaspoon of soda. It fizzed while I drank it and the bubbles went up my nose. Sometimes we'd walk up the Sleepy Hollow ditch that was full of 3' and 4' ledges that had pools of water. Each rock had lichens and lots of mosses and small ferns. We'd pick up odd-shaped rocks and stones and bring them back to add to her rock garden along the house, which contained some perennials and always a few marigolds.

Lucille was short and stout and probably the most friendly lady I ever met. I use the word "lady" deliberately because she'd always stopped to talk or walk with me. I could describe her best by quoting Thackery's *Vanity Fair*: "She was a good-natured mistress pursuing, quite unsuspiciously, her bustling idleness."

Floods

June was strawberry time. For two weeks, Mom would fry pancakes and, before turning them over, she'd add a generous covering of strawberries. They were served on a platter topped with a thick layer of sugar. They were hard to make because the berries would stick and burn easily, but we wolfed them down. Sometimes Adeline and I would make our own little strawberry treats by beating strawberries with sugar and egg whites and then take it to a secret retreat to be eaten with spoons.

We loved to go barefoot, and each spring we kept harassing Mom to let us do so. Her response was there were to be no bare feet until the lilacs bloomed (early to mid-May). Soon, the bottoms of my feet became tough and I'd walk on the gravel road, on thistles, around the farm and hillsides and only put shoes on to go to church or visit our rellies. My feet developed a mind of their own and rebelled at being constricted. We did put shoes on for haying as the hay stubble was sharp and cut our feet.

Floods were exciting for us kids but not for adults. Adults had to repair ditch fences, pull logs out of corn fields or the meadow hay, clean up debris and repair ditch crossings. To get equipment to the sand hill fields, the ditch banks had to be cut down and smoothed on both sides. Flood water was full of silt. As it went over these ditch crossings, the silt was deposited on both sides, making a dirt ledge, sometimes 4' high, which was too steep to cross with a wagon. We'd take the team and use a scoop to fill in the bottom of the ditch if it had been scoured out; then we'd taper the banks and move any excess silt away to make a smooth crossing area for our hay wagons.

Floods would take out ditch fences from the neighbors upstream and deposit them in our fields. It was one-hell-of-a-job untangling the wire from the mud, logs, branches and other miscellaneous debris. And yes, we'd find bottles, cans and junk from the ditch dumps of the folks upstream!

With water chest-deep and squishy mud between our toes, we would walk across the fields and flooded meadows. We floated toy boats made with the draw shave from the shop tied with a long twine. After one flood, Willie cut a birch pole about 18 feet long and about an inch and a half around. He showed me how to vault across the sand hill ditch that was full of racing run-off about eight feet deep. He was good at it. I waited until the water had receded a bit and found a narrow spot. Sometimes I landed short with wet boots. This meant more skunk grease when they dried. Dad cooked out skunk fat for shoes which kept the leather soft and prevented it from cracking. It did work. After a few days the smell was gone, unless we got into a really warm room!

"Dad cooked out skunk fat for shoes which kept them soft and prevented cracking."

The Woeful Ones

On a warm day, bicycle riding was great fun. Along with Donnie and Robbie Sip, we'd ride together on old off-road trails or over the road banks. We'd race, slam on the brakes and spin 180 degrees. In spring, we'd raid neighborhood rhubarb patches. We'd drop a teaspoon of salt into our pockets, ride down the road, then crawl on our bellies over to Hawkinson's rhubarb patch, steal a stalk, then crawl back to sit in a wet washout along the bank. Great criminals. I can imagine the Hawkinsons watching us and laughing. Later, we extended our criminal activities to stealing strawberries. However, this required putting sugar in your pocket. We even stole out of our own patch, which was fun for Donnie and Robbie as they didn't have a strawberry patch.

In June we'd search the hillsides for patches of dewberries. They looked like tiny strawberries and were very sweet when dark red and real ripe. The large ones were about half an inch in size and had pointed ends.

July was the time we picked black raspberries. We knew where all the patches were. We found several bushes of golden yellow ones growing wild. It was our guess that they were escapees from early settlers and had their seeds spread by birds. Mom would make pearl tapioca pudding and cover it with black raspberries and sugar. It was so good we all would have eaten more if it had been available.

The Woeful Ones. Milt is in the middle.

One year Robbie and I planted our own watermelon patch. We fenced out an 18' x 30' patch below the road about two blocks from Sips' out of our cow pasture. Using a horse and a single cultivator we prepared the patch. We hoed. We cultivated. We even carried water. We watched them come up, first the vines, then the melons, bigger and bigger. September came and, alas, an early frost and dead vines. We analyzed and decided to cut some open only to find them a very light pink inside and not yet edible. "The best laid plans…" We had planted too late near the end of June. The patch faced north and had fall shade. 'Twas not to be the last disappointment in life.

After big rainstorms, we'd always meet in the back pasture between our two homes and play for hours. Floating sticks downstream, wading across, sometimes cutting long sticks and vaulting across, often ending up in the water. Once we were wet, anything went. We'd take off our clothes so they could dry if there was any sun or wind. We'd have mud fights, smear ourselves with mud, stand on the bank and see who could piss the farthest (Donnie always won.) We'd look for new debris that had washed down and special rocks that had been recently exposed. As the ditch slowed to a trickle, we'd look up and say, "Gosh, it's late," put on our clothes and run for home, in my case catching hell for being late for chores or supper. In Donnie and Robbie's case they never had a set hour to eat and more than likely they'd have to make their own supper, heating up beans with a piece of white Red Owl store-bought bread, costing 8 cents a loaf.

Donnie and Robbie's dad had a workshop that was a paradise of junk and rarely had room for his coupe. Every time I went over, they would be making something different. They were always hammering, bending, sawing and making toys or trailers to pull behind their bikes and boats to float in ditches. One time they made a cart with four metal wheels from an outcast one-cylinder engine. They used rods for axles that were drilled on both ends. Because they had no money for cotter pins, nails were put through the holes and bent to keep the wheels on. The cart box was 16" x 30" with a 2x4 nailed to each end. The front had a second 2x4 bolted loosely under the box so it could be turned by pulling on ropes attached to each end. The front and rear axles were stapled onto the bottoms of the 2x4s with fence staples. The driver simply tugged the rope from one side or the other to turn the cart. We pulled it uphill on the county road, but, alas, it never worked well on gravel. So we took turns: one would ride and another would pull and run like the devil.

We made long-handled T-bars and used them to run the iron retainers from the hubs of large-spoked wagon wheels. They were ½" wide and 12" in diameter. We would roll them up and down small rises, across ditches and along the road. We started by hand-rolling the circle to get it going, then guiding it with the T-bar. Whoever tipped his disk first would lose.

We were very inventive kids and the junk piles held endless possibilities! The fun came in the creation. Some of our inventions were quickly abandoned to litter the yard to wait to be recycled into another project.

We rolled rocks down the hill across from their house in our back pasture. We carried old tires to the top and, as they rolled downhill, they'd bounce high in the air. Sometimes, Robbie crawled inside a tire and Donnie would push him down the road or off a bank. We walked along barn rafters 20 feet above the barn floor to destroy English sparrow nests. With our sling shots we shot at everything imaginable: trees, signs, old bottles in the ditch, a rock in a puddle; but telephone insulators were our favorites. Who could shoot a rock the furthest? The highest? We always argued who was right or who was best. We had no money, no purchased toys, but that made little difference to kids with unlimited imaginations.

Donnie and Robbie had a rat terrier who was always in a family way. We had fun playing with her little pups. Mutt was her son who got his name from Gim, who never held a high opinion of Mutt or his parentage. One time their dog lost all her newborn pups and was fresh with milk at the time several newborn piglets were motherless. Donnie and Robbie taught them to drink at different fountains. Eventually the dog-pigs and Donnie and Robbie got their picture in the *Red Wing Eagle* newspaper.

Milt practicing his archery skills. Note: there are few trees on the hillsides.

Mutt's Glory

In the Spring we trapped pocket gophers whose hills or mounds were damaging to farm equipment, earning 10 cents a piece. We'd dig down near the dirt mound and tunnel under it until we found the "T" in their runway. After that, we cleaned out the soil and dug a depression so the trap would be flush with their runway. We took the fine, moist dirt off the mound and almost completely covered the trap, making a level walkway to the pad that would spring the trap. We cut a circle of sod and placed it over the hole and pulled soil around the edges so no light would enter. If we did everything right, our success ratio was about 75%. Later in the year as the gophers learned our trapping techniques, it dropped to 20%. I recorded each trapped gopher and date in a book to present to Dad at the end of year. We usually sold some hogs or cattle during the late fall at the South St. Paul livestock market. I'd wait until the hog or cattle check arrived in the mail to present my bill! I remember one year during the Depression when the price received for the hogs sold did not even cover the cost of trucking them to market!

Gopher mounds were hard on all machinery, especially mowers and rakes and made loading hay tricky if you were high on a load and a wheel went over a mound. If this happened on a sidehill, the whole load could slide off the wagon! A horse could break a leg stepping in a woodchuck hole, so we waged a constant war against them as well. Our dog Mutt was our number one woodchuck eradicator. He'd tree them and bark. If his bark came from the meadow, I knew it was a bull snake; if from the woods, it was a woodchuck. I would walk up the hill, climb the tree, crawl out on a branch and shake the woodchuck onto the ground, or poke it with a long stick. Mutt would grab the woodchuck by the neck, hang on and shake and shake. He became very proficient at doing this and killed some as big as he was. I don't remember him ever getting beat up or even bloodied. When I bought a 22 caliber rifle, I'd bring that along, and if they were too high up in a tree, I'd just shoot them. That was no fun for Mutt and he gave me that "What did you do that for?" look. "I've been barking here for 2 hours." One summer Mutt and I got 28 woodchucks.

I tell these stories just to point up Mutt's glory. He also loved to kill rats in the old mill or when we

Mutt as a puppy with Lucille Broze, Milt, Dora and Adeline.

moved piles of corn. In his formative years he was bitten on the lip but he soon learned to avoid that fate. We'd usually call in our cats for the smaller jobs like killing mice, although Mutt—if he had nothing better to do—might stoop to do that job. He had the bad habit of chasing cars. He was not good at that task and never brought a car home! A fish peddler from Bay City hit him and sent him to that faraway doggy land.

The fish peddler came around in the summer driving an old coupe with the trunk enlarged to hold ice and fresh carp and catfish. Mom always bought fresh catfish and smoked carp. It was so different from our home-cured meat. We were crazy about his smoked carp and considered it a real treat!

Years later, in 1990 at our Maiden Rock farm, Marilyn and I walked over to the ski shack and our neighbor's dog King followed us. He surprised an old woodchuck in a brush pile and did battle with it, getting more beaten, than beating up. Both combatants would stop and puff and then continue. After about 20 minutes, King was bloody all over and I said, "King, you'd better give up." The three of us wandered back toward home, but when we got a block from Sid's, King wanted to go home with us. He looked toward his house but knew he would not get past Grace into the house and she'd give him holy hell. I said, "King, you might as well face her. Go home." He understood and did!

Another time, I had a big woodchuck in my Maiden Rock farm machine shed, so I enlisted Bob Sand and his big German shepherd. It took her half an hour to dispatch the woodchuck and just barely! But she was a city dog.

Lilacs

We always had a flower garden that was handed down from sibling to sibling. I inherited mine from Adeline and we tended it as a joint venture. She liked to grow gladiolus and bought special new bulbs. We'd go up on Hawkinson's hill and pick up a bucket of sheep manure and water it down for a few days, then pour it on her glads. Adeline won Grand Champion in the Red Wing flower show at the Armory. The success of these beautiful blooms was the result of two or three liberal applications of sheep manure tea.

My garden had Canterbury bells, nasturtiums, zinnias, pansies, marigolds, and glads. It was my "Home Beautification" 4-H project. I thought, why fool around with animals? I did that all year. Sad to say, I never took it very seriously and year after year recycled the same projects. I had a flower bed, helped with the garden and planted a birch or basswood every spring. I'd redo my yard drawing every year, take a bouquet of flowers and my diagram to the County Fair and put it in the Hay Creek 4-H booth. At best, I got a red ribbon, but nothing more.

When I was able to drive, my 4-H career abruptly ended. Merlin Holst and I delivered a cake for the meeting and then skipped out to go to Bay City. The next morning Mom asked me about the meeting and I said, "Oh, the same kids got re-elected: Strauss, president, Stump, VP," and so on. Three days later, a different report came out in the semi-weekly newspaper and all hell broke loose when Mom read it. I had to confess. Who-wee! That was the end of my 4-H experience.

Every Memorial Day, Red Wing had a parade and a service on Levee Park by the train depot. We never attended. The WWI Veterans and American Legion marched with Major Loy and his horse leading the parade. They shot off rifles and placed a wreath on the waters of Old Mississippi in memory of lost sailors. Each year a different local preacher was chosen to say a prayer.

Red Wing also had an August parade during the Flower Show when Adeline won the Grand Prize. One year, I made a two-wheeled trailer out of a wooden Winesap apple box. I used old wagon wheels on a rod mounted under a cross piece. A board stuck out the front and I drilled a hole in it so I could draw a wire through and attach it to my bicycle's kickstand. I'd give Janet, my baby sister, a ride down the road. Even if it was so rough her gums would knock together, she liked it and fussed when the ride ended.

When it was suggested to put us in the parade, my sisters wrapped crepe paper around the box and the handlebars on my bike. Janet and I rode all around town without her fussing, as she sucked on a little glass mirror from Mom's purse. Several times, good-intentioned ladies warned me of the dangers of her chewing on glass. After having birthed five children who had wended their way precariously through all the childhood hazards without serious mishaps, Mom was not concerned about the sixth chewing on a mirror!

"Our yard was well-maintained by farm standards. Most farms had peony bushes and scraggly beds of yellow iris. We had perennial beds on each side of the long walk from the driveway to our front door."

We got our picture in the Red Wing newspaper but got no prize. That was my first and last public appearance. I wanted to try out for the high school plays, but I didn't have the courage.

Our yard was well-maintained by farm standards. Most farms had peony bushes and scraggly beds of yellow iris. We had perennial beds on each side of the long walk from the driveway to our front door. The beds were full of Columbia roses with low, ever-bearing yellow button flowers, daisies and other perennials. Near the drive were two circular beds, one of roses, the other of phlox whose blossoms were great for picking and sucking out the sweet liquid. Near the top of the sidewalk were several flower bushes. To one side was a large bed of tiger lilies. It was always fun coloring up our hands with their pollen, or drawing a mustache, or better yet, sneaking up behind a sister and marking them. Two circular beds of petunias and geraniums had 16" ornamental wire fences around them and were saved overwinter. A large double mock orange was planted near the cow tank to hide it and a hydrangea was in the opposite front corner. Dad or Bob made a six-foot high ornamental trellis for the climbing rose bushes. In the front of the house we had spirea and near the kitchen window was a passion flower with its exotic blossoms. For a number of years, Edith grew an 8-foot bed of sweet peas tied to a 6' diagonal wire. When they were in bloom, daily she placed a bouquet on our table.

It took the efforts of 3 or 4 family members to maintain all these beds. The ground was dug up in the spring and composted manure was added. During the summer, weeding was a constant activity. Each fall, the roses were laid down and covered. Visitors marveled at our flowers and that made Mom proud of our combined efforts.

Eventually we created an extensive fencing project along the front yard by the driveway. First, a rock and cement footing was laid upon which a rock and cement wall about 16" high was built. Steel posts were embedded every 8 feet to hold the wire fencing about 60" high with space left for a center gate. When it was finished, we planted lilacs, including a French lilac, along the fence on the lawn side. These were the bushes that determined when I could go barefoot. I often thought of pouring hot water on them so they'd bloom earlier!

> The Metropolitan Opera came to Minneapolis every spring during the third week in May, and for nearly 30 years Marilyn and I would walk from the parking lot on the other side of University Avenue to Northrop Auditorium to attend. As we passed through a quadrangle of lilacs in full bloom we'd dally, smell the fragrance and enjoy the brilliance of the blossoms, recalling our childhood flora memories.

Above the lilac was a Hayslip crab whose fruit was pumpkin-shaped, about the size of an English walnut, that turned dark red when ready to pick. The apples were extremely sour but very flavorful when baked with sugar and cinnamon. They had much more flavor than our other crab, the Whitneys, that were so sour even the worms didn't bother them!

Fourth of July

The Fourth of July was always a great time. Over the year I'd save the 25 cents or so plus any money I'd earned from Gim for weeding her asparagus bed. My goal was to buy a bag of fireworks at Enz Sporting Goods in Red Wing. The asparagus bed was 50 feet long and 6 feet wide and each year was topped with a load of manure that brought new weed seeds! After agreeing to work for 50 cents, I finally cajole Gim into giving me 75 cents. I bought Cat's Paws which were small firecrackers woven together in packs 16" long. I bought rolls of caps for my cap gun and round red balls that exploded when we threw them on a sidewalk or against a cement wall. We burnt "snakes" that left a long grey residue, like a snake. We had sparklers, larger firecrackers and skyrockets of various varieties. When I got older, I bought really powerful cherry bombs.

Blowing up cow pies was a favorite sport. The goal was to blow up a cow pie behind someone without getting splattered yourself while running away from the explosion. Cow pies got so scarce in the barnyard, we'd follow the cows around and wait. Sometimes, the back of my shirt was all splattered green. Mom should have been angry but she'd let things like that pass so her brood had a little fun.

With Donnie and Robbie, we'd throw the red round ones inside of the new concrete bridges to increase the noise. Fun with firecrackers took imagination. We placed fireworks in holes, under cans, in trees, in barrels, on wood chips, in the water tank, down the old cistern, in pipes with one end plugged and in the tailpipe of a car. We'd drop one in a tobacco can and quickly close the cover. We put them in snuff boxes, down a mouse hole, in a squirrel hole (starting a tree on fire), in the handlebars of our bikes, down a rain gutter and down a drain pipe. This listing only scratched the surface of all our possibilities.

Donnie and Robbie had expensive 6-shooter cap guns with individual six-shot tabs. Mine had a roll that unwound as I shot and was not as loud. The rolls would always stick and break. I always envied their 6-shooters, but one had to choose! Donnie and Robbie always shot up all their goods long before the 4th. I'd save mine!

When the circus came to town, "there were days of excitement and anticipation before and awesome memories after." Goodhue County Historical Society Photo.

Cherry bombs could blow a can way up in the sky and break the sides of the can. They were packed 50 in a box and would have taken most of my meager earnings. During this week, our dogs and cats went into hiding and made themselves very scarce, never trusting mischievous boys!

Willy liked to show a picture of what he said was me having a temper tantrum on the kitchen floor. Don't you believe him. That was my cousin!

To Willy's dismay, Dad told the story about how Willy locked himself inside a small storage room that he couldn't release the catch and get out so he bellowed, hollered and cried. They found him hysterically shouting, "I'm dying. I'm dying. I'm DEAD!" Bob put a ladder up to the window, crawled in and opened the door.

If you look closely you can see mom in the background ignoring me.

A Swarm of Bees

Our most-used piece of furniture was a 2" x 10" oak plank bench that was 6' long. It had two clay supporting tiles on each end. The clay tiles were added after the new smokehouse was built. On some summer evenings the hired man, Dad and Mom would sit on it as the sun drew its golden chariot under the earth, making its nightly trip.

Grandson Andrew Hayman works a hive of bees. Notice two queen cells left center that needed to be removed to prevent the hive from swarming.

On summer evenings, we'd watch and listen to nighthawks calling, circling, catching bugs with their sharp, erratic moves. We listened to a neighbor's cows bellow, dogs bark, heard the muffled sounds of someone working late or someone shouting directions to a child or a dog. Sometimes a whip-poor-will would perch on our stone retaining wall near the horse barn and serenade us with its plaintive call. We listened to the frogs, smelled the perfume of the lilacs moving on a slight breeze, sensed the coming meadow dew and drew in the smell of the day's fresh-cut hay, that in its own way was as fragrant as any flower. Finally, the mosquitoes would drive us indoors and to bed but not until we'd watched fireflies and tried to capture a few in jars. Samuel Butler understood: "All has long since vanished and become a memory, faded, but still fragrant to myself!"

In June we hassled Mom to buy root beer extract that was peddled by the Watkins traveling salesman. When he came around, she'd buy several square, 3-4 ounce, clear glass bottles with corks in them. Us kids willingly helped scrub the quart bottles with a bottlebrush and cleaner and then carefully rinsed them. She added only sugar and water to the extract. Thirty to forty bottles were capped and put in the cellar to age for a week or more. More often than not, we couldn't wait that long, and after a few days we'd get a bottle or two to cool in the cistern! Although it had not quite aged, in a kid's mind it was very delicious.

Later, brothers and sisters took to hiding bottles around the basement, creating their own private stash. Once in a great while they'd forget a bottle and, where it exploded, it left the tell-tale sign of broken glass around the secret enclave. Once in a great while, Mom would serve root beer to our company. We didn't like that at all, especially if they were relatives. Serving neighbors wasn't as bad.

I believe I had some of this brown, sparkling beverage when I was very young. I was out in the playhouse with my sisters and maybe some friend, or cousin, Betty or Lois Peters. Before I was born, Dad decided to build a 9' x 12' house to store his beehives over the winter. Sad to say, this never worked too well because the bees always developed diseases and died. After he gave that up, the girls cleaned the room out and decorated it for their new playhouse. They put an old piece of worn linoleum on the floor; the cabinets they used for their tea dishes were apple boxes. They had a towel thumb-tacked over the top of a small table and used chunks of wood for stools.

Occasionally I got invited to one of their tea parties. I didn't look like a romantic French courtier, with holes in my pants and bare feet, but I attended because there were special treats the girls made. When a shortage of "bodies" existed, a Shirley Temple doll occupied one stool. Being close to the flower garden, a small bouquet was always centered on the table in a cracked old jelly jar.

As a young'un I hated bees. One day I used a big stick to beat on the cover of a hive and angry bees poured out. Mom heard my terrorized death scream and met me halfway from the house beating bees off of me. We both got stung many times. I spent an agonizing night, as there was no place on my body that wasn't stung and hurt to lay upon!

When we saw a swarm of bees, we'd beat on the bottom of a pail or tin, or hammer on an old brake drum. The goal was to make the bees land nearby so they could be caught and re-hived. We didn't really know if this was a rustic myth or if there was some validity in doing so. We did notice that most of the time they did settle nearby.

An old rural saying:
> A swarm of bees in May is worth a load of hay.
> A swarm of bees in June is worth a silver spoon.
> A swarm of bees in July isn't worth a fly.

Can you find the queen?

Bob told a story of how one Saturday he and Willy captured a mother skunk and her five babies. The skunk had sprayed the dogs as they dug out the skunk's hole. They took a piece of barbed wire and twisted it around in her fur to pull her out. One stepped on her head while the other tied her onto the end of a 10' birch pole. The babies came out of the hole to follow mama. They could be picked up without getting sprayed. They took them home and quickly built a cage of octagon wire and put mama inside with her young'uns.

Can you imagine any mother with five infants allowing herself to be tied onto a pole without fighting back with every resource she possessed? Mom made Bob and Willy leave all of their clothes outside. They scrubbed in an old galvanized iron washtub but the odor was embedded in their skin.

Sunday morning as they sat in the warm church pew, the skunk's odor started to spread around. The neighboring sinners started to stare at Bob and Willy. Bob, realizing this, got nervous, fanned his hands in the air, and sweated more, which made the smell even worse. It could have been the only Sunday Mom was damn glad to have the service end. They didn't wait to shake hands with the preacher but bolted with all speed! That was the last time Bob went to Mom's church.

And what about Mama skunk and her babies? They spent a very short time in captivity. Mama broke out and they all quickly disappeared.

Willow Bush Farm

Talking with Normie and Howard Hawkinson, our neighbors kids down the valley, Bob and Willy found out a circus had been in town. Bob asked Dad about that and he said, "Oh, you're too young." That didn't wear well with Bob as the Hawkinson boys were about the same age. It would have been better if Dad would have said it was too expensive.

I remember the first of two or three circuses I attended. There were days of excitement and anticipation before and awesome memories afterwards. Nothing more impressive ever happened during my childhood. Mom took my sisters and me and gave the ticket man a $20 bill and he gave her change for a ten but wouldn't give her the difference. Losing $10 was a great hardship and it sure ruined her afternoon. These were Ringling Brothers Circuses, as Barnum and Bailey played bigger cities.

Sometimes on Sunday afternoons, Donnie and Robbie and I would ride our bikes down to Wells Creek to swim in a deep hole under the bridge. When flood water wasn't able to get under a bridge fast enough, it swirled around and scoured out a hole. We swam, played in mud and sand, dragged a big log into the creek and dove off it, had water fights and caught frogs. We made use of and had fun with anything that was in the area. If we had any energy left, we'd ride over to Floyd's Tavern for a bottle of pop, but that was rare because we never had any money.

Summer entertainment was going to a ball game. Not a major league game like the Minnesota Twins versus the Milwaukee Brewers but local teams like Hay Creek versus West Florence. Although sitting watching a game was not much fun, for a few hours it was a get-away from the farm. Bob and Willy played catch in our yard in the evening, especially after they came into their "big money."

Their "big money" was a result of someone telling them to grow big yellow popcorn. They ordered seed from a specific seed company and Dad agreed to give them an acre just as long as it didn't interfere with their other work. That acre was the cleanest, best-kept acre on the farm. In fall, they shelled it and ran it across a screen to clean the chaff. They had small success trying to sell their popcorn in Red Wing until they came to Frederick and Kemp. The Haymans were well-respected by the Fredericks. Art Johnson, who later became Willy's father-in-law, checked it out. It popped well, so they bought their entire crop for $124. Willy and Bob were in pig heaven, or at least in corn-no-money heaven. That crop gave them a new lease on life's happiness!

Bob said he never had so much money. Bob bought a new glove and an old used Indian motorcycle. Willie bought a mitt and a shotgun.

Occasionally we'd take a drive into Wisconsin and picnic along Lake Pepin or watch a ball game at Maiden Rock and buy pop at the little stand. Sometimes Dad would drive to a park in River Falls that had the biggest bottles of root beer anywhere. I could hardly drink it all at one time! These picnics usually ended in a park near a lake or river or creek, a setting we never tired of.

With no year-round creek running by Willow Bush Farm, we were drawn to go to places with water for fun and relaxation. The farm was named for the diamond willows that grew along the ditch by the sand hill. You could easily carve out the diamonds with a jack knife and they made colorful walking sticks.

Next to the willows was our

Bob on his Indian motorcycle he bought from the proceeds of raising yellow popcorn.

watermelon patch. In the spring, manure was scattered over the surface with a pile to be "worked in" later to fertilize the individual melons and Hubbard squash. This was one cultivating and hoeing job we did not mind, because with sandy soil and a south-facing slope, the site grew excellent melons. In the fall in the mid-afternoon, when we were working near the patch shocking corn, we'd stop and use a jackknife to cut up and share a melon or two.

It was 1936 when the Rural Electrification Act (REA) installed poles and strung wire to our farm. Dad and Bob started wiring the house, barn and machine shed, so we had working electricity in all major buildings by the end of 1937. Dad and Bob spent many months fishing wires through the walls of our house and making connections. The outside buildings were easier and faster because they were all open and wires were simply attached to posts and beams.

This improvement revolutionized farming. Gradually we got electric motors for almost every job. Big motors for the grain elevator and pump jacks and smaller motors that were moved from job to job for the fanning mill, corn sheller and numerous grinders. With electric lights, we could see what we were doing, especially during short winter days. Trouble lights helped us repair machinery in dark places. Finally, we got our first efficient tractor. Together, these two changes significantly impacted both our way of farming and our quality of life.

Later on, wires were run to the hog house for heat lamps for the baby pigs. When we wired the chicken coop, with the light on during winter evenings, the hens laid more eggs. No more setting clucks. We now had electric egg incubators and electric water heaters! Eventually farm equipment came with motors already installed, which led to farm machinery with built-in internal combustion engines. Over the years we benefited from other improvements such as batteries and rubber tires.

Wilbur bought a shotgun with his "big money." His pet crow made it harder for him to sight it in!

Early School Year: District 90

District #90 School was located about a block from the intersection of Hayman Valley and the Hay Creek Valley. The school stood 1/6th of an English league from our home. Note, I've said English, as opposed to French. Rabelais explained why leagues were so short in France: "At every spot where they turned their girls on their backs they were to set up a stone—and that should be a league!"

Normally we walked the road to school, but sometimes we cut through the pastures if both the Hawkinson's bull and our bull "Big Business" were of a friendly disposition. During my tenure, the school was populated by the Fluegers, Michelsons, Dierks, Horns, Sipelmeyers, my sister Adeline, and two families of Holsts. Adeline had problems with the meanness of some of the older students, but in most cases she handled it pretty well.

Four pictures hung on our school walls. The ever-present George Washington with his screwed-up jaw rumored to result from tooth problems. Another was of "Honest" Abe Lincoln with his country-rustic face. The two others were a painting *The Gleaners* and a picture of farmers pitching hay onto an almost filled hay wagon. I felt Washington and Lincoln, two great men, were appropriately wonderful models. But why pictures of country life? We spent our summers doing farm work and that's all we knew. I wonder why our teacher did not try to broaden our horizons with pictures of the Alps or wonders of the world?

Entering the school house were two cloakrooms, one for the boys and the other for the girls. Each had a window. The main classroom had six large windows. Outside was a woodshed and two toilets, one on either side of the school, at modestly correct distances.

The school was in the center of an acre of ground. On one side was a small cemetery surrounded by a 2' high decorative wrought-iron fence and four large well-spaced white pine trees. Ten members of the Rose family who had ended their God-fearing lives of toil and tears were buried there. The cemetery was unkempt with only a few yellow day lilies adding a last tribute to their memory.

During my first few years in school I was protected by my sister Adeline. These were the small desk, Dick and Jane years. After inspecting my coloring, it didn't take my teacher long to recognize that I'd never out-distance Raphael. Dark was good. Two minutes using green. Two minutes using red. Two minutes with yellow, then brown. Done. When I went over the lines, I'd draw a new line in black! I'd press so hard my hand got hot and my crayon would snap. In less than one month my whole box of new Crayola crayons were all broken.

The most fun was cutting out and decorating Christmas trees. We made Easter baskets by cutting construction paper in strips and closing both ends. These were glued in a circle and crushed down to flare out in the center. We'd plug the bottom and glue a bright-colored handle over the top!

Making Valentine boxes was just as fun, although the experience could be cruel. Sometimes classmates gave nasty Valentines or skipped a person they didn't like. Who had the most? Who had the best? Our parents made sure the teacher received nice big pretty ones, but somehow they never seemed to fit.

Our school teachers usually stayed only a year or two. Marie Johnson was pedantic and left no loopholes for opposition to her program! After her came Georgia Van, who could be manipulated into a program her students thought wiser, at least from the standpoint of work required. Many others came and went.

I survived the tricky meanness of some of the older boys. Achilles' famous words ramble about my brain: "I hate that man like the Gates of Death who says one thing but hides another in his heart" (Homer's *Iliad*). They could be great friends one day, but evil lurked in their minds.

Regarding school, I followed the Scriptures, Psalm CCXXVII, "It is vain for you to rise up early." I ran or rode my bike like the wind from a cow eating fresh alfalfa. The school bell rang at 9 AM. When I arrived late again, I thought about another Rabelaisian: "Early to rise brings little wealth, but early drinking's good for the health." Red wine, anyone?

In second and third grades we studied spelling, reading and began arithmetic. Merlin Holst joined us and Marie Johnson had a hell of a time getting him to put the Hs into his broken English. Donnie and Robbie Sip joined us for a while and then left for the parochial school in Hay Creek, 5 miles away. They took a horse and buggy to get there. Why they left, I don't know. I missed the Sips because while at #90 we'd walk home together and plotted after-school strategy.

Charlie Sip bought 40 acres from Bill Miller for $1000 and paid it off by working for them. 80% of the Sips' garden was cabbage to make sauerkraut. The cabbage was cut up and placed into a 100-gallon clay jar and left outside to freeze. They'd scrape it out with a hog scraper. They usually ate kraut, potatoes, and, in fall, squirrels. So the three of us would hunt for their meat. Donnie was old enough to handle his dad's rifle but seldom had any bullets. Instead, we'd use an air rifle, which made it much harder to kill a poor squirrel and lowered our success rating. Usually, we cleaned out the surrounding hills of squirrels for their family dinners!

One time I got into a fight with Donnie and Robbie. As I left I shouted at them, "Your place looks like shit, you've got shit all over the place and you're shitty too, you shit, shit, shit!" Well, this got back to Loretta, their mom and she told Lucille Broze who told my mother. I was taken

School District 90. Imagine going to school in a building with no lights, no running water, no fans or air conditioning! Water was carried in from a farm a ½ mile away. Heat was by a pot bellied stove. After completing the eighth grade, you graduated from a country school and either went to work or on to high school in Red Wing.

Edith graduated from high school at age 16. After one year of Teacher Training she began teaching at School District 113 along Hay Creek where she was younger than her oldest students!

At the time, these were some of the rules for teachers: not to marry or keep company with men; be home by 8 p.m. and not to loiter downtown; not to ride in a carriage or automobile with any man unless it's your father or brother; not to smoke cigarettes, wear dresses with bright colors or dye your hair. The school room was to be swept once daily, scrubbed weekly and a fire started by 7 a.m.

"Edith would often play games with me, and our favorite was Monopoly. Although she usually won, I enjoyed playing with her. She was always pleasant, upbeat, friendly and probably the best of all of us."

to task and told this was not the kind of behavior God expected of me. In a few days, we were back hunting together.

I always felt sorry for Donnie and Robbie going to school. In the winter, they wore only a light jacket with no hat, maybe gloves or maybe not. They had little beat-up lunch buckets that contained two slices of white bread with beans one day and sliced onions the next. No apples. No cookies. They usually ate their sandwiches at recess and had nothing left for lunch. Then they'd maintain a macho "we're not hungry" attitude. Occasionally, if I had 3-4 cookies, I'd give one to Robbie.

We'd play kitten ball at recess and over the noon hour. The teacher often came out and played with us. She maintained a degree of order and fairness for the wee ones.

Another game we played was "Annie, Annie Over." The woodshed was the divider. One team on each side of the woodshed and a small rubber ball was thrown across. When caught, your team split and ran around each side of the shed. The other team did the same but didn't know who had the ball. The catcher threw the ball and tried to hit a person on the other team before they got around the shed. The person that was hit was then on your team. Of course, there were arguments. "I hit you." "I didn't feel it." Often, someone on your team would peek through the shed's wood slats to see who caught the ball and which way they were running. When you knew that, you could run around the opposite side.

Bill Holst liked to toss the ball over the school. It was more difficult and he was the only one able to catch it. He'd throw the ball so hard it would hurt, especially for a little first grade girl like Marion Dierks, a cute little puddin'-headed kid with reddish brown hair, bangs and BIG brown eyes.

Bill was Bill Jr. or Bill the second and his son, Bill the third, was just as tough and mean. He was in the demolition business in St. Paul. His men were non-union when three union boys came around to "talk" to him. He said, "Come on over to my car, boys." He opened his trunk, took out a baseball bat and started swinging. Then they decided to "let" him finish the job. One time he was in the Gas Lite restaurant on Hwy 10 in Wisconsin and some cop smarted off to him. Bill decked him and then called the Sheriff's Department in Ellsworth. He said, "Come on over and pick up one of your men. He's lying on the floor over here." This story is on the record. He didn't even mind paying the fine.

In late summer, our neighbors cut the long grass around the school just before it opened. We'd collect it and pile it to make grass houses. We'd put a few boards over the top and use more grass to make a roof.

Fourth grade was time for book-reading competition. I was in a race with Russell Holst. Our teacher kept a bar graph chart on the wall showing our progress. He'd get the teacher to allow him to read 3rd grade books that he could read fast. I read a lot of books that year, and for my prize I got a piece of Red Wing Pottery that I still treasure. It was a brown striped gopher leaning up against a football. It was meaningful because Russell and I both followed U of M football with a great quarterback, Paul Giel, a kid from Winona.

I liked reading interesting text books. I remember a colored picture of a train traveling on a track to the moon that said it would take 90 years to get there!

Each week the *Weekly Reader* was mailed to our school. It contained a composite of weekly current events with photos. It was an excellent educational tool. We'd have to report on one article or subject in front of our class. Too often some smart-ass would make faces at whoever was giving their report.

When the Holsts brought a football to school, we'd play a shortened, back-alley version of the game moving the ball in any direction. We'd argue what was legal according to our own, ever-changing rules. We'd come back into school hot and sweating only to find the water cooler empty. Our teacher would say, "Sit down and work," and then instruct one classmate to go up to Hawkinson's and get another pail of water. We'd kill a half hour waiting and drinking and would have to give up math for that day.

The smoothest con we ever pulled was on Marie, our teacher. It lasted for a while and extended our lunch hour into 1½ to 2 hours. This gave us time to wander farther out onto the hills. The school bell was rung 5 to 10 minutes before class was to start. We'd hear it and amble in. There were some times on beautiful autumn or spring days

"The smoothest con we ever pulled on our teacher was when someone quietly crawled up to the belfry tower and inserted a 16-penny nail through the center of the rope and into the last board the rope went through," extending our lunch break by 2 hours. Goodhue County Historical Society Photo.

that someone quietly crawled up to the belfry tower and inserted a 16-penny nail through the center of the rope and into the last board the rope went through. When the teacher couldn't pull the rope or ring the bell, we'd come back an hour late. Marie would be mad as hell and say, "Didn't you know it was late?" We'd say, "We were having so much fun, we forgot about the time." The truth was, we'd spent our time discussing how much longer we could get by with what we'd done.

An enterprising student would offer to crawl up in the belfry to find the problem. They would pull out the nail and leave it near the hole for next time and advise, "The rope got caught between a steel rod and the floor" and reported "they'd bent the rod down!" Marie would accept the help because she didn't want to bother the school board for help. We were smart enough to wait several weeks or sometimes a month and do it again. This time we'd say, "You pulled the bell too hard and it swung over and caught the rope." Next time we'd explain how the rope got caught around the arm handle.

Finally she smelled a rat and forbade anyone to climb into the bell tower for any reason. We had to send someone up one last time to get rid of the nail so a school board member would not find it. We accomplished this during an afternoon lesson when someone had to go to the outhouse or he'd wet his pants. The rest of us would keep her attention with little problems, so she wouldn't look out the window!

Winter was a time for playing fox and goose. This was a game with a large pattern in the snow, like a wagon wheel. We'd run along the spokes into the safety of the center circle, because anywhere else you could be tagged. Then you were "it." Another pattern was a spiral with a "Free" or "Safe" center with two snow barricades. We'd pick sides and have snowball fights. If you hit someone, they had to come over to your side. Some of the older kids made their snowballs hard as rocks.

Students had weekly jobs to help the teacher, because the school did not have any janitorial services. Every day, two students carried water from Hawkinson's milk house, located half a mile away across the valley. Two more hauled in firewood. The little ones clapped erasers or dusted the teacher's desk. The desk monitor walked around to check if every desk was in order and reported on those that were not. Two swept the boys' and girls' cloak rooms and the main room. We all got to polish the floors. On Friday afternoon, a sweeping compound was

Edith and Adeline dressed warmly to walk to school. "One exceptionally cold week in January, Adeline and I were the only ones in school. During that time the outside temperatures ranged between 25 to 35 degrees below zero."

scattered across the floors and we all skated up and down the aisles for 10 minutes, sliding and polishing with our shoes. The boys all had knee-high leather boots and sometimes a nail would stick out and scratch the floor. As the Holsts moved about, they stomped around like little Prussian generals.

One exceptional cold week in January, Adeline and I were the only ones in school. During that time the outside temperature ranged between 25 and 35 degrees below zero. We did not stay home. The school was as cold as charity itself. We hovered around the stove and warmed our feet on bricks we'd heated on top of the stove. That week we read a lot. Although I wasn't a great reader, we had a considerable number of American and English classics in our home. For Willy and Edith, "This little library was like a small oasis in a desert and they learned to drink deeply."

During recess in bad weather we'd play word games. For example, how many words can you make from the letters in *Christmas*. Or we'd play hangman, battleship and tic tac toe.

Spring meant snow melting and the formation of a 3' deep pond behind the school. It provided endless entertainment to run and slide or play hockey with a frozen cow pie. The ice would get soft, and the game turned into who would be the last one across before breaking through. Melting brought high water in the ditch. Many a day in March some students would sit near the stove and dry their pants and boots.

Later in the spring, we'd go up the hill and roll rocks down. Some of us would be a little bit down the hill with a smaller rock in our hands ready to try and stop the bigger rocks as they rolled past. We were always looking for bigger adventures. The rocks got bigger, until one day a big rock got away, jumped the fence, crossed the road and slammed into the side of Marie's well-kept Model A. Marie had a trigger temper and was mad as hell! The rock-rolling adventurers stayed after school longer than normal!

My longest record time for detention after school was 6 PM. It took a little figuring out how to handle Mom and my undone chores! It all started when we saw a great big bull snake curled under a rock pile. We pulled off the rocks, tore the pile apart and dispatched the snake without mutilating it. I don't know who came up with the brilliant idea, but we carried it down to the schoolhouse. We lucked out, as Marie was in the ladies' sitatorium. We opened the top drawer of her desk, curled the bull snake nicely in a coil and propped its head up with its mouth open so it could look up at "Teach" when she opened her desk.

When District 90 School was closed in the early 50s, the building and its contents were sold at auction. The big black school bell sold for a few dollars and was later purchased by Dad for a few dollars more. He kept it for some time. Marilyn told him that she was interested in the bell, but he sold it to a man in Pine City. Marilyn wanted that bell, found the owner and paid $60 to retrieve this memento that was once on the school where both Dad and us kids got our early education. Another antique worth saving!

As the afternoon went on, we thought she'd never open her desk drawer. We tried to create some reason for her to reach in. We could make an error so she'd need a red pencil. Tissue? Wrong drawer. Rubber eraser? Her answers varied. "Leave the mistake." Need a paper clip? "Bend the corner." Ruler? "Where's yours?" Finally! She opened her desk drawer, and we never heard such a scream in our lives. I bet Hawkinsons heard it a quarter mile away.

She was a well-challenged teacher and hung in there longer than most. I'm sure she had an ulcer before she left us. We talked her into and out of more things than Hamlet and Horatio could think of.

During the Great Armistice Day blizzard (11/11/1940), we stayed in school until 3:30 PM. We had worn only light jackets, no hats or gloves. We rode our bikes home on icy roads where you couldn't see through the snow and terrible wind. These were the times Mom worried about us. Neighboring farmers who had been out plowing with their teams of horses simply unhooked their plows and returned home. The plows remained frozen in place until the following spring! Twenty-foot snow drifts were reported near Willmar in central Minnesota. The blizzard left 49 people dead in Minnesota and killed thousands of cattle.

Arguments were a source of entertainment. The Holsts were Republicans. Adeline and I were Democrats. We'd argue and exchange slurs about WPA and CCCs doing nothing more than leaning on shovels. We argued about John Deere tractors versus Minneapolis Moline, about brown Swiss versus short horns, about Dodge versus Studebaker and German shepherd versus collie. "My dog is better than your dog."

Ginnie Flueger became an irritation. Already in grade school, she was turning into a beauty. Don't know how many hours of learning I lost lusting after her.

There were the Michelson boys and another heavy-set boy that always smelled of cow manure. We called him "Big Barn Smell," something out of Al Capp, no doubt.

One of the few jokes Dad told me was about a one-room country school. The young teacher was working late. Johnny was standing behind school with an erection. He was putting navy beans on the end of his peter, drawing it down, flipping beans over his shoulder trying to hit the window. Apparently with some luck, as the teacher was watching she became

A Civilian Conservation Corp (CCC) camp located nearby in Hay Creek resulted in a lot of conservation projects being completed in the area. Dikes were built to control erosion and retaining walls for roads and bridges. Goodhue County Historical Society Photo.

aroused. She opened the window and said, "Johnny, get in here immediately." He did and she gave him further instructions! Afterward, she asked, "Johnny, what'd you think of that?" He looked down and said, "It was okay but you ruined my bean shooter!"

Sometimes I went over to the Holsts on Sundays. They'd built a clubhouse out in a pasture with a door that locked. Each one of the three had his own box of treasures inside with a lock on it! They always had more candy to eat than I ever had. I couldn't figure it out as their family had a smaller farm. Their sister Margaret was always nice to me and the only one who married well.

Some say school was the best time in their lives but I can't concur. I was happy when I graduated 8th grade. After a special ceremony in Wanamingo, I got my diploma. This was important because many farm children never went any further in school.

School District 90 was organized in 1862. The settlers in the community held a meeting to organize the school and each subscribed a small amount with which to put up the building. The names of the settlers were as follows: T. Godard, Bennewith, John Hack, Anton Scharf, Ferd Scharf, Peter Stromberg, David Bartron, Wm Issensee, Anton Zignego, H. W. Cady, Manny, Wm Hayman, Jake Turner, Wm Miller B. Moser, Wm Goodell, C. Johnson, Wm Damas and Wakefield.

There was a donation from the Rev. Bishop Whipple who was then bishop of Minnesota

The amount subscribed was $80.00. This sum paid for the materials. The labor, no doubt, was donated.

The schoolhouse was finished May 5, 1864. A teacher was hired for 20 dollars a month and he boarded around, two weeks at each home.

The lot, which consisted of one acre, was donated by Daniel Saunders, whose farm joined the lot on the north.

The Grange, a farm organization, held its meetings in this school. A barn was also erected in which to house the settlers' horses while attending meetings.

Items for expenditures on this building quoted siding at $13 per M and shingles at $1.75 per M.

In 1886 the new building was erected at a cost of $700.00 and again most of the work was donated. Wm Miller did the carpenter work and received the old building, which he moved to his place and added to his home.

When the building was finished, Anton Zignego said, "I am going to buy a bell to put in that belfry," and he presented it to the school.

An Episcopal Sunday school was held in this building for a while which was called The White Lily Sunday School.

Nimrod, The God of The Hunt

Hunting was a big part of rural life. First we used a slingshot and then an air rifle to shoot sparrows and cowbirds and even cows that wouldn't move to the barn when asked politely. As an early teen, I used a 22 caliber rifle with a peep sight, 6-cartridge clip with a solid walnut stock.

I got my first shotgun when my college roommate, Bill Engebretsen, invited me to Frazee, Minnesota, to duck hunt on a three-day weekend. I rushed out and bought a single shot shotgun with a plastic barrel which kicked like a mule. I'd shoot and miss or worse, just wing one. Bill had a double barrel Damascus twist. He'd shoot and a duck came down with both feet pointing straight up towards Heaven.

Back then, a family could be fed with a shotgun and rifle. By the end of February when the family was out of meat, a deer was shot in the late afternoon. They'd take it in the basement and the whole family would work at cutting it up and processing it. By late evening it all was cleaned up. They were always afraid a neighbor might stop by in the morning and they wanted everything to look completely normal.

Mrs. Engebretsen never washed her cast iron frying pan. At lunch, we would find traces of breakfast in our food. Same for supper. Dinner, the main meal, was always at noon. I felt she never liked me because she thought I was the sinner who turned her son away from the Bible. She was mainly right. One night Bill read me all the sexual passages from the Bible. He knew exactly where to find them, and I thought his mom shouldn't have blamed me entirely.

Nimrod was the god of the hunt. "Willy bought a Remington 12 gauge, semi-automatic shotgun. He was a deadly sure shot."

Willy bought a Remington 12-gauge, semi-automatic shotgun. He was a deadly sure shot. Every fall, he hunted pheasants and grouse with cousin Emory, Maggie's son. Emory had worked all summer for Adolph and Alfred Peters and spent all his $100 savings on a new Browning, fully automatic rifle. When his parents found out how much he paid, they were mad as hell.

In winter, we hunted jack rabbits on the prairie near Bellechester with 22 caliber rifles. We shot up boxes of shells jumping those big jacks on the other sides of low ridges. We'd bring home 4 or 5. We'd take a broad ax and chop them up for the cats. Willy claimed it was the most fun of any hunting.

December 7, 1941, we were hunting squirrels over on the sand hill in a warm, light mist. As it was late in the season, we only found a few squirrels looking for a few nuts their cousins may have missed.

"For pleasure and melons want the same weather!"

One sunny October weekend, Bill went home and when he returned a few days later, he was putting a poison ivy salve on his jewels. A week later he heard that little Cindy had similar crotch problems. I chided Bill for being so stupid as to roll around in a poison ivy patch!

When I returned home, the radio was blaring away. The Japanese had attacked Pearl Harbor and FDR declared War! It was a day I would never forget.

Emory went into the army. When he came home, he told Willy that on the rifle range the recruits shot so badly that the captain reported it to the commanding officer. "But," he said, "there's one kid who's really good." The commander wanted to see him shoot and Emory shot three bullseyes in a row. The commander said, "Make that man a sergeant!" Emory was killed in the Battle of the Bulge.

Willie and Tom Comstock were both fast and very competitive pheasant hunters. You'd hear only one shot and each hunter would query the other if they had shot, too! The funny part was, at the end of the day, Tom's dad divided up the birds. He lifted them and gave Willy the heavy ones. They were the ones full of lead. So much for the fine camaraderie of the hunt.

During the war, Bob got a 30 caliber Army Carbine in exchange for a quart of booze. When he came back in 1946, we used it to hunt deer, which had just started moving into our area. We chased the poor animal over hills and across three farms before it dropped and lay dead by Willard Holst's. We put an ear of corn in its mouth and when Willard came out to look, we told him we caught it eating his corn and shot it with the cob still in its mouth. Willard was amazed.

In drought years, squirrel hunters trespassed on the back of our farm without our permission or knowledge. They'd try to smoke the squirrels out of a hollow tree. Late at night we'd see the whole hill on fire. We'd all go out with wet, old jackets and shovels and spend hours putting it out!

Bob was a navy pilot during WWII and served as a carrier pilot. He received honors for sinking a Nazi submarine in the Atlantic off the Azores.

After the war ended, he served as a flight instructor at the Ft. Lauderdale Naval Air Station until 1947. He participated in the search for the "Lost Squadron, Flight 19," five Avenger torpedo bombers which disappeared over the Bermuda Triangle area on December 5th, 1945.

While living on the east coast, Bob flew for Pan American for 26 years.

Hired Men

The hired men in the 30s were an interesting lot of eccentrics, misfits or others that were simply out of work. They fell through the cracks of society and lived and moved to the beat of their own drummer. They'd come and go as they pleased. Sometimes they left for no reason at all or because they didn't like the next task at hand. They'd leave without warning, go on a three-day drunk, then, out of money, sometimes they'd come back, sleep it off for a day in the barn and then get back to work.

One of the hired men, Jim Hamer, spent time with hobo companions on Washington Avenue in Minneapolis. Come summer, he'd come to the farm to work but he wouldn't milk or sleep in the house. He slept on a cot in the barn. One time Willy and Bob tossed rotten potatoes through the barn window at Jim who was lying in his cot. Jim tore out of the barn and just missed catching the two delinquents.

Jim spent winters working in a Northern Minnesota lumber camp and told many interesting stories about camp life. He told about the big sleds they used to haul logs out of the hills to the frozen rivers and how they laid strips of hay to slow the sled of logs while going down hill. Jim also talked about riding trains.

Cap Real, aka Big Bozo, liked beer. Part of the time he lived in Red Wing above some cheap bar. He told us about the whores on Second Avenue in Winona and the "ladies" of the St. James Hotel in Red Wing. Bob and I disagree on his ever helping with the milking. He liked to split wood, load manure and do field work. Of course he had some bad habits, but he bought fireworks and often gave me candy. We became great friends. I'd get water for him and he'd let me sit on his lap in the big wooden rocker, a secure retreat.

Cap and I were tossing split wood into the wood shed when Kate Miller walked by us on her way to the outhouse up the hill just above us. Cap would holler, "Where you going, Kate? Whatcha gonna do, Kate?" She'd go back into the house sputtering to Mom about Cap, "He doesn't sweat it out his sides." Cap liked to catch her coming around a corner with the chamber pot and say, "Whatcha got there, Kate?"

Cap talked about one of the skeletons in the family closet. Typical of the time, my great-grandparents lived with my grandfather and his first wife, Sarah. Gin was a young girl working for the family when Sarah died. He (William Jr.) was in his 40s. According to Cap, one of the hired men discovered the two of them together on the floor of the old mill. 'Twas ever thus.

Oscar Adams was an out-of-work car salesman and was accused of bigamy. Turned out he applied for a divorce but never paid the attorney. As a result, the attorney never filed his divorce papers.

Big Albert dug pine tree stumps out of our front lawn. It'd take a day to chop off all the roots, then we'd pull them out using a team of horses. Big Albert slept in the barn. He'd work for meals and snuff and when the job was done, he got a pint of whiskey!

Little Bozo (Milt) with Big Bozo (Cap Real). "The hired men in the 30s were an interesting lot of eccentrics, misfits or others that were simply out of work. They fell through the cracks of society and lived and moved to the beat of their own drummer."

Ed Hanson was a fireworks promoter. He'd bring a whole bag after a drunk. In the evening, he'd sit on the bench and watch the bigger kids shoot them off and the little ones run around with sparklers. One Sunday we came back from a dinner and Dad found Ed stinking drunk lying behind the cows in the gutter where they do you-know-what. To quote Rabelais, "He tossed it down like a theologian…there wasn't a burrow in his whole body where wine didn't ferret out his thirst." Dad pulled him out and he slept if off in the hay until the next day.

After that, Dad boarded up a corner in the basement under the stairs. He put all the wine barrels inside and a padlock on the door to discourage any hired men from future temptations. Later, I discovered I could remove the board under the top step, drop into the wine cellar and help myself. I'd stack two barrels together to crawl out, replace the board and put the nails back into the old holes. Adeline was often a co-thief!

Two of our last hired men were Germans. George Furste was an East Prussian. The other was "Old Chorch" from Bavaria. These two men hated each other's guts. Chorch said George, "Ran around like a fart on a curtain rod." The main reason for the hatefulness, according to Chorch was Prussians put Bavarians in the front lines in the heat of battle. Dad finally told them they'd have to quit fighting or they'd both have to leave.

According to Willy, George Furste was an educated man, but Bob said he had no common sense. Dad finally sent him over to Claus Quell who spoke his language. He swore at him in German and he worked out well over there.

George got up at 4 AM. One time he suggested changing the fencing and the main gate on the road so we'd never have to stop the car or team to open a gate. Dad wanted to move the pigs from the pigpen out to another field that was a good distance away. Knowing that pigs are not easily herded, George said, "That's easy." He took a 12' length of rope and tied on 6 or 8 shorter strings, each with an ear of corn tied to the end. The boys took the rope ends, George opened the gate and the hogs followed the ears all the way over to the new feeding ground.

We had a hand planter for corn and beans, but George had trouble making it work. Dad practiced with him on the front lawn: down; open the handles; pull out and close the handles, until he got it right.

George liked to go to the Hawkinson's and play Bunco, a dice game, with them. Before he left, he converted all his wages and savings into one dollar bills and left with a huge roll of money! He got a job in Chicago working for a steamship company. Years later, Tom visited him and his son in Germany.

All these men had interesting stories to tell. We have forgotten most of them. It would be interesting to know their fate. This was a time when most men were too proud to go to a county old-age home. Hopefully, Roosevelt's New Deal helped pick them up.

George Furste was a hired man who returned to Germany and whose family have kept in contact with our family. These men all had interesting stories to tell.

Yellowstone

With few exceptions, vacations were almost non-existent. When Dad got a new Champion Studebaker, it provided an opportunity for us to travel. Mom and Dad, Willy, Edith and Adeline went to Yellowstone National Park. They had a great time providing many memories. Mom bought me a little leather coin purse with *Yellowstone* and a picture of a bear on it. Bob stayed home to tend to the farm. I helped Cap haul wood. Gim over-saw the crew of three and helped milk and cook.

Besides one fishing trip to Mantrap Lake in northern Minnesota, Dad, Gim and I went up to Port Arthur and Fort Williams in Canada to buy woolen long johns (with a drawbridge). Dad always claimed he couldn't find good wool in this country. It was great being away from the cows for three days. The only high point of the trip was to climb Mt. McKay, an old metamorphic, vertical uplift from the Laurentian Rise that towers 600' above Lake Superior. We ate cooked beans and corn beef sandwiches and staples from home that cost very little!

One time, Gim took me overnight to St. Paul. We rode a train and a street car. We stayed at Mrs. Nast's and ate dinner at the Golden Rule lunch counter. We had roast beef and mashed potatoes for 25 cents each and finished with a dime sundae. We saw a movie at the Paramount Theater which was much bigger than the H.B. Sheldon Theater in Red Wing. After the movie, I couldn't find the Men's, so Gim said, "Come into the Ladies." Well, when I was near-relieved, two 55-year-old ladies came in and thought that a 12-year-old was much too old to be using their sacred domain. I got a good earful for doing that!

Gim often bought a 2# bag of giant cashews and stashed them in her roll-top writing desk. I'd get hungry for cashews and discovered if I sat on the center of the desktop, my weight would bend it enough to slip past the lock. I'd swipe the goodies and re-lock the desk. Gim never did figure out why the roll-top went down.

When farm work piled up, Dad would go into a funk and tell Gim he couldn't come up with money for taxes, etc., etc. Gim would go to her little black tin box and get $200. The farm was left to Gim. Dad only owned Sleepy Hollow. Gim got the money from selling the milk and butter in Red Wing. One year, Dad told her, "I can't make it. I'm going to quit and get a job in Red Wing." He had five mouths to feed. She agreed to give up the milk and butter money. Dad stayed.

We did business around Red Wing with Swanson Hardware, the Feed Store, Hanson and Gustaphson Grocers and Josephson's Clothing. We were rarely ever paid "in full." When we sold hogs or beef, we'd go around to each store and pay a little down. With H & G Grocers, we bartered with eggs. They liked Mom's eggs because she'd wiped them clean. If the bill went too long, a merchant asked for their money. No one ever charged interest on their outstanding bills.

Once in a great while we saw a movie in Red Wing or heard a free band concert. In Dad's younger years, he'd go down to the Villa Maria in Frontenac to see summer Shakespearian plays.

Edith, Adeline, Bob and Willy spent late fall and winter evenings playing games with the Broze girls. Our favorites were Pit and Authors which sponsored much shouting, hollering and cheating until late at night. Rook was another favorite and the edges of the cards were all worn and bent. Old Maid was the first game I learned and the girls would play it with me. Our usual night treats were popcorn popped over open furnace coals with melted butter, home-grown apples and occasionally cookies or candy.

One Christmas our family got a new board game with pockets in each corner. It had a hollow center, two short cue sticks and red and green disks. The object of the game was to sink your disks in the pockets. It was great fun and had other games on the back.

Edith would often play games with me, and our favorite was

Monopoly. Although she usually won, I enjoyed playing with her. She was always pleasant, upbeat, friendly and probably the best of all of us. She dated Ernie Walters, a well-liked fellow from Lake City. They liked to roller skate. He brought her flowers, and one Easter he gave her a live Easter Rabbit.

Our favorite radio programs were *CAPTAIN Midnight* and *Jack Armstrong, The ALL-American Boy* adventure series. We'd send in a cereal box top with 10 cents and get the Hike-o-Meter just like Jack used on his radio program. We'd clip it on our belts to measure how far it is to school or any store. The challenge with it was you had to bounce up and down when you walked to get it to work. When Jack was in Egypt he used a secret code ring while exploring the tombs. It was a must-have item. We developed our own codes with our friends so no one else would know our signals. The whole American Boy series was developed by a cereal company to market their products to American boys!

One Christmas our family got an electric phonograph and records of Vienna waltzes, "Wine, Women and Song," "Tales from the Vienna Woods," and the "Beer Barrel Polka." Finally we had music in our home, albeit on plastic disks.

When there was nothing else to do, there was always good old Cat and Rat, at home and at school. We had a Magic Slate where we wrote words that disappeared when we lifted the plastic sheet. We also played Pick-Up-Sticks and carefully used one stick to remove others from the pile.

Thanksgiving Dinner was "special." Gim got a goose from her sister, Mrs. Quell. She'd stuff it with a sage and raisin bread dressing. We had roast goose, mashed potatoes, at least three vegetables, cranberry sauce, apple and date salad. Our relish plate was full of pickled crabapples and homemade baby dill pickles. Mom's pumpkin and mincemeat pies had flaky crusts and were made with lard and loads of cinnamon, nutmeg and allspice. They were served with dark brown, vanilla-flavored whipped cream. Our lord Appetite reigned for the day. The gods resided here, as much as in palaces full of delights.

"With few exceptions, family vacations were almost non-existent." When Dad got a new Champion Studebaker, it was an opportunity to car camp to Yellowstone National Park.

Vignettes

There was the story about when Mom brought Little Willy home from the hospital and laid him on the couch. A short time later she heard him crying and found two-year-old Bob beating the b'jeebers out of him.

When I was born, Dad was up north fishing. Oscar Hawkinson drove Mom to the hospital. Ho-hum, number 5 has now arrived!

Imagine bringing a live pine tree into the house for Christmas, decorating it with candles and lighting them! One time Adeline's dress brushed against a burning candle and her skirt caught on fire. She ran, but luckily someone grabbed her and rolled her in a rug.

Seasons came and went without too many problems. Bob and Willy had their differences and chased each other around the circular table in our living room. Adeline and Edith argued who did the baking last week and who did the cleaning.

Gim referred to Willy as, "The little runt who would never amount to anything."

Mumps, measles and chickenpox circulated in winter and spring.

Dad never subjected himself to keeping hours. He felt hours were made for man and not man for hours. This irritated Bob to no end because he wanted to get the jobs done. He became restless, desired more and wanted change. He saw nothing but drudgery, hardship and despair down the road of farming. Farming prospects made Bob unhappy; besides, there were younger brothers.

Willy had the patience and perseverance that Bob lacked for farming and made a success of the venture.

Our first Studebaker car, purchased in 1916, had Izen-glass curtains. The front seat passenger had to hold the gear shift handle to keep it engaged. This inconvenience energized Dad to raise 100 hogs that he sold to get enough money in 1926 to buy a new Dodge Touring Car for $1200, complete with everything on it.

The Hayman home was on a main Native American path to Red Wing. Grandfather said a white man couldn't walk in the same path easily, since Native Americans put one foot down directly in front of the other.

Great-grandmother told how Native Americans stopped at the farm for salt to add to the carrier pigeons cooking in a pot near the house.

"The Hayman home was on a main Native American path to Red Wing. Grandfather said a white man couldn't walk the same path very easily, since Native Americans put one foot down directly in front of the other." Several family members remember seeing a photo of three teepees at the toe of the slope below the Hayman home. Jack Bratrud's drawing attempts to replicate that memory.

Another time they stopped for molasses. She gave them some. Soon they were back for more. When they came to the door the third time she showed them the jug was completely empty by turning it upside-down. When no more ran out, they were satisfied and left.

Grandfather told the story about when he was a small boy. He and his Father were at Batron's helping dig a well. Toward evening, his father sent him home to do chores. On the way, a couple wolves started to move in on him. Although he had a small 22 caliber rifle, he had only one shell. He was smart enough to know a wounded wolf might also be bad news. He fired his gun into the air. His father heard the shot and sensed there was danger, grabbed his gun and headed for home. He saw the boy and the two wolves. He shot one and the other ran away.

In the early years, there was little timber near the farm. The reason was that Minnesota Sioux burned the prairie to provide better habitat for buffalo, one of their primary food sources, as the fire killed young trees. The Wisconsin Ojibwa did not follow this practice. As a result there was plenty of wood in Wisconsin. In winter, great grandfather and grandfather would take a team down to Frontenac and cross the ice into Wisconsin to cut firewood. The area was probably right below our previous home in Maiden Rock.

One day, they cut until about 3 in the afternoon then loaded their sled. Grandfather's dad asked if he would stay and cut wood till dark. "You can sleep in Zignago's hut where there's a chunk of meat. Go ahead and cut a piece off." The shack was built into the side of the hill and had a

"The early farm had a state-of-the-art windmill that turned a corn sheller, had a grindstone and ground grain. People came from miles around to see how it worked. The 1916 photo shows the wooden windmill and the hills just starting to grow over with timber."

The Pipe Shall Lead Us Known and Speculation
by Nephew Joe Deden and Mary Bell

Known: The pipe was gifted to William Hayman Jr. (Milt's grandfather) by members of the Prairie Island Indian Community. He was the first pipe bearer in our family. I remember seeing a photo of the Hayman homestead with the distinctive windmill and the house on a rise with three teepees in the valley at the toe of the hill where the Haymans used to garden(Confirmed by Marilyn Hayman, Niles Deden and Dan Hayman).

Charles Hayman (Milt's dad) was the second pipe bearer in our family. During the 1960s, Charles taught his grandchildren to make kinnikinick-Indigenous tobacco. I remember spending a hot summer gathering red osier dogwood bark, sumac bark, corn silk and mullein leaves which we dried and then smoked. He also taught us how to load the pipe honoring all seven directions, praying for Mother Earth with multiple rounds of prayer while smoking the pipe and honoring our ancestors. He taught us the saying, "Mitakuye Oyasin," which basically means all living things are related. He turned and carved the crane pipe stem currently in use. I do not know what happened to the original stem. I have been told the stem is sometimes buried with the stem maker/user. The pipe is always passed forward to another generation.

I, Jerome Deden, am the third pipe bearer in our family. Grandpa Charlie passed the pipe on to me in the early 1970s while I was in college. I had the pipe bag made from a moose hide that we shot in the BWCA. The pipe was blessed and taken into sweat lodges as part of ceremonies. My wife Mary and I took it to the American Horse/Afraid of Bear Sun Dance outside of Lead, SD, in 2018. Mary took the pipe to an Ojibwa Women in Water ceremony near Hayward, WI, in 2019. Our quest has been to learn more about the pipe, pipe ceremonies and where the pipe originated. An eight-page document details our learning process.

Known: the pipe was quarried in Rice Lake, WI, where a Catholic church was later built. The pipe has lead inlays made from lead bullets. The front design of the pipe represents otter tracks. Other designs represent arrow fletchings. There are six bars on the pipe representing the six directions (N,S,E,W and above and below). There is a circle around the upper bowl representing spirits within the 7th direction. Etchings on the flat base surface are a travel log representing the pipe's original journey. Because of its large size and complex design work, the pipe was a ceremonial pipe.

Speculation: The Sioux Uprising occurred in 1858. Around that time, members

of the Sioux nation were making pacts/treaties with surrounding tribes/nations. The pipe was used in a ceremony between the Sioux and Ojibwa nations and was held by a member of the Prairie Island Indian Community. As is often the case, animosity existed between tribes/nations and at some point this ceremonial pipe was gifted to my great-grandfather.

A Diné (Navajo) friend said, "The pipe shall lead you." Traditionally, a pipe ceremony leader would need to practice for years with an elder. Now, shamans say that the Earth and our civilization is in great peril and the ceremony should be held by anyone who is willing to step in. The ceremony itself will become the teacher and let you know immediately if your intentions are pure. This process is a combination of honoring our ancestor's wisdom from many different cultures and creating our own process of connecting to a source of healing.

hole in the ceiling to let out the smoke. While he was cooking the meat, he looked up and saw six pairs of eyes looking down at him. The wolves smelled the cooking meat and him! He kept the fire going all night long and didn't sleep much. The next afternoon, when his father asked, "Would you like to stay and cut more wood?" he declined.

I remember as a child of 3 or 4, hearing the eerie night sounds of wolves howling on the sand hill bluff and our dog barking back. The howl of a wolf has always been something that makes the hair on the back of my neck stand up! It is a very primordial sound.

The early farm had a state-of-the-art windmill that turned a corn sheller, had a grindstone and ground grain. People came from miles around to see how it worked. The 1916 photo of the farm taken at night shows the great, wooden windmill and the hills just starting to grow over with timber.

Charles Hayman. "In the 40s, Dad took up rural electrical wiring and years later wired our new home. By then he'd mellowed out and was doing work he was more suited for."

Bob, Willy, and I, along with our wives, visited the home-site of the Tappelaski's in Northern Wisconsin. Dad bought wine and beer from him during the Prohibition years (1920-1933). Tappelaski was an old moon-shiner. One time he was picked up by the Feds. They found his moonshine buried in a sawdust pile. After that, he was very careful and told buyers to leave their money in the hole of an old oak tree and come back later for their moonshine. He buried some "shine" in his garden. He'd count five hills of beans, then dig down and pull out a jug of moonshine. He told Dad he had a barrel buried under the cement slab in the bullpen. He was waiting for it to age and the price to rise. Later that winter, Dad heard he and his wife were asphyxiated from some kind of a malfunctioning stove.

Willy told the story to the two fellows that owned the Tapppelaski's place. The barn was gone but the cement slab was still there. Willy wondered if they found the barrels after they rented a jack hammer and broke up the slab. It was probably a moonshiner's story to entertain a couple of young boys.

Willy said Wisconsin never ratified the 18th Amendment, which declared the production, transport and sale of intoxicating liqours to be illegal, so the state and county never enforced it. Many moonshiners moved from Minnesota to Wisconsin, including some on the 10 acres grandfather owned under the Red Wing high bridge. Between them, squatters and hookers, grandfather had so much trouble they finally sold the land for little or nothing.

One spring, one of Willy's kids' college friends planted a 4' x 8' patch of marijuana in the cornfield by the sand hill. He liberally applied a 50# bag of fertilizer and the weed grew about 3' above the corn. Willy dang near got an ulcer watching it all summer. The grower sold the crop for around $400. That was the first and last time as far as Willy was concerned.

As a child I found Dad was often a hard, fearsome person to live with. When he was building the smoke-house he had a mortar box filled with ready-to-use cement. As a tyke of 5, I saw others throw sand into the box, so I picked up a small handful of sand and threw it into the cement. Dad saw that and took off after me. He caught me on the other side of the house and really spanked me. Too often he took his frustrations out on me.

In the 40s, Dad took up rural electrical wiring and years later wired our new home. By then he'd mellowed out and was doing work he was more suited for.

Charles Hayman in Colville Park, 1970. He died in 1977 at the age of 84. "He liked to tell stories about Tappelaski, an old moon-shiner that Dad bought wine and beer from during the Prohibition years (1920-1933)."

Dora Hayman
by sisters Adeline Deden and Janet Golisch

Mom was a hard worker and had a busy life raising her six children. She often milked cows and had to do the milk dishes. The chickens were hers. She set the hens to raise new chickens to eat and for layers. She had a big garden with Gim. Fresh bread was baked every other day. Besides her children and Gim, they had a hired man, so there were many hard-working, hungry people to be kept fed.

About all the food she bought in the grocery store was flour and sugar; all the rest of our food was either canned, dried, smoked or stored on the farm! In the basement was a hoard of food from our summer's labors. It varied by year but generally included: 80 half gallons of beef chunks; 50 half gallons of ground beef (hamburger); 80 to 100 quarts of sweet corn, green beans, beets, stewed tomatoes and tomato juice; and 60 to 80 quarts of wax beans, a pea and carrot mix, sauerkraut, peaches and pears. In addition there were small jelly jars of various jellies and jams and pint jars full of sweet and dill pickles, as well as pickled beets. All this was canned on a wood-burning stove during the heat of summer!

Mom had to bake bread and cookies for our school lunches and for the three daily meals. Her raisin coffee cakes were the best. When she wasn't cooking, there was milk that had to be run through the separator as we sold the cream or churned it into butter. The skim milk was fed back to the livestock. After the milk was separated, the machine had to be cleaned and the shotgun milk pails washed in the back kitchen as we had no milk house attached to the barn.

Mom didn't like the fact that Cap, the hired man, drank a lot. Each time Dad would hire him to load the huge pile of manure by the barn, Cap would throw his hat into the kitchen while standing outside the door. "You didn't throw it back out, Dora, so I guess I can come in," he would say.

"Mom was a hard worker and had a busy life raising her six children. Beside her kids and Gim, they had a hired man, so there were many hard-working, hungry people to be kept fed."

High School and College Years

During the war years (WWII), Merlin Holst and I would go to the Hay Creek Store and buy two pints of ice cream and root beer. We'd go up the creek, swim and eat our "sodas." During that time, cigarettes were scarce. At the store, Mrs. Borkhart would only sell Merlin 15 cent Avalons. He knew she had both Camel and Lucky Strike cigarettes under the counter, which she kept for her best customers. This made him angry and he stole punches off the punchboards and often won a cheap box of candy.

One summer we decided a diving platform would be fun and we

"In 1947, Dad and Mom built a new home in Sleepy Hollow. Wilbur married Francis Johnson and they moved into the farm house."

spent two weeks building one out of his dad's clear used lumber. One Sunday afternoon, we took it to the creek, crawled on and immediately it sank to the muddy bottom! Alas, it did not hold even one of us. We had many ill-conceived ideas with no parental direction and—being too scared to ask for help—we kept many of our projects secret.

Another wild time was when we ran Willy's hay wagon around the barn yard on Halloween. Art Johnson, Franny's dad, stuck his head out the door and called, "What's going on out there?"

Merlin and I would talk on the party line evenings and we knew two or three busy-bodies were listening. We'd tell impossible stories and create scandals: a neighborhood girl was pregnant; someone had an accident; another lost his job, all unnamed, all part of our imaginations. It was our little *School for Scandal*.

In a rural school yard in the Wells Creek area, we tried to take down the flagpole. Both of us were pulling on the rope when the pole broke and hit Merlin on the head. It would have killed an ordinary kid, but not Merlin, although he had a headache (probable concussion) for several days.

One New Year's Eve we went to a dance in Zumbrota. We'd picked up two girls with substantial foundations. Merlin was driving his small, two-door '36 Ford down past the Boetcher's farm when he reached over to plant his lips on the chops of the young lady next to him and drove off a steep 20' embankment. I was in the rear, necking with my girl, and our heads hit the ceiling when the car slammed down and bounced. Luckily the car stayed upright. Merlin hit the gas and with a foot of snow under the car he drove a quarter mile down the field and back onto the road. We stopped for several minutes and sat there laughing. I was glad I had my arms wrapped around that young woman or I could have broken my neck when I hit the ceiling.

The next morning the neighbors saw the tracks in the field and for two or three days it made for great discussion about who made them. They never did find out and realized they'd missed something unnatural.

One November, Willy and Fran were in Iowa City for a Minnesota/

Iowa football game when Vince (Deden) and I hunted deer all day without any luck. Around 3:30 we were standing on the sand hill point figuring we'd covered everywhere, which meant the deer must be in the neighbor's unpicked corn just west of Willy's. Vince stood at the corner and no sooner had I walked into the field when three ran out. Vince shot one. That presented problems as we couldn't leave the deer and couldn't drag it and leave a blood trail in the snow, as hunting season was closed!

The deer must have weighed 150 pounds and we took turns carrying it on our shoulders. When we got to Willy's, we dropped it on his hayrack and blood drained onto the boards and into the snow. We took it over to Sleepy Hollow and hung it in Dad's workshop. Next morning, Willy came out to haul hay to the cattle and saw the blood. He ran up to the house and called Mom on the party line. Of course, she couldn't say anything on the phone and simply told Wilbur that he should come over. That didn't make Willy any less upset. He had some agonizing minutes between his place and Mom's front door!

One April Fools Day two fools, Bill Engebretson and I, had been wandering around the countryside most of the night looking for trouble. Around 3 AM we decided to stop at Vince and Adeline's. For some reason Bill had his trumpet along. Trumpet in hand, we entered their house, opened the upstairs door and Bill let out one of his more persuasive blasts. It took Vince a few seconds to recover from his paralysis, come to the top of the stairs, turn on the light and shout, "You crazy fools!" Then he went to the other side of the house and explained to his folks, who lived there with them. We thought this was

Milt shoveling snow from Gim's house in Red Wing. "I had four blue-collar-type friends. We played poker and drank ginger ale. Two blocks from Gim's house was a skating rink where we met our friends."

so much fun we decided to try it on Willy and Fran, but their doors were locked. All we could do was blow the horn, but the delight was minimal.

Grandpa William must have drunk some bad hooch. For three nights in a row he dreamed of "Gold" under a big rock back in the hog pasture. The 5-foot high rock was bigger around than our dining room table. Off went Willy and Bob with shovels and picks. They dug and picked, then dug some more. Eventually they had a hole under the rock that was the size of a shipping carton for an overstuffed living room chair. For days their dreams of what they would do when "rich" fueled their enthusiasm and strengthened their muscles. Eventually, they came to the inevitable conclusion that it was only a dream. No gold and back to reality!

One day Bob and Willy noticed a blue jay nest on a branch in the big white pine. The jay is not man's most friendly bird, unlike their petite cousins, the sweet-singing bluebird or the bob-o-link who warble and chortle with such joy as they fly over the hay fields. The jay could learn a music lesson from either one. Us boys climbed the pine to check out blue jays' nests. Nearing the nest, the two parents attacked us with force, digging their talons into the top of Willy's head.

So Bob went up to the attic and got Grandpa's old World War I army helmet. Willy strapped it on, climbed back up to the nest and the jay came down and banged into the metal. It was quite a humorous event. Willy held on as the jays took turns diving on the helmet, not willing to give up to the enemy of their chil'ens.

World War II and high school occurred simultaneously. During the first year we took turns driving to school. One week we'd drive and the next we'd ride with Bill and Russell Holst. That winter I spent the three winter months in town and stayed with Adeline and Janet Schafer in Gim's house on South Park street. I went home on weekends to work. My sophomore, junior and senior years, I drove the Studebaker Champion to school and regularly hauled cream to the creamery.

Milt, Janet and Wilbur. Janet was born in 1939 and was 11 years younger than Milt and 19 years younger than Wilbur.

I had four blue-collar-type friends. We played poker and drank ginger ale. Two blocks from Gim's house was a skating rink where we met other friends. Ray Campbell drove a Model A with a rumble seat. He was a good influence and helpful in extracurricular activities. Tom Featherstone, Albin Dickey and I often ate lunch down by the levee. If we really felt wealthy, we'd stop at Nord's Drug Store and order cherry malts for 35 cents. A double cost 45 cents and ended up being 2 ½ large glasses because a gal from the class ahead of us worked there.

Occasionally we'd stop at the Palace of Sweets for a grilled cheese sandwich. It was frequented by the jocks and the sons and daughters of Red Wing elites. Being farm kids, we never felt very welcome or comfortable there. Unlike Lake City or Zumbrota, Red Wing was more status conscious. It was the same at the Youth Center located in the YWCA basement. It was set up for school kids with a jukebox and pop machine. We didn't dance, so we'd have a Coke, watch for a bit and leave. All city kids could dance. Usually a party was there after a home football victory.

One time I got involved with the jocks for a bit. Our '41 Chevy pickup came in handy for the homecoming parade. We decorated it with crepe paper. Our slogan was "Roast the Raiders." Scot McGrew turned a crank on a spit where a football dummy went round and round. The dummy was a "Raider" of course.

During my junior year, I helped decorate the gym for our semi-formal Junior/Senior Prom. Again, Dad's pickup was brought into play. We drove into Wisconsin over to the prairie near the Red Wing airport and cut four large pines from a windbreak to use for decoration. We drove back at breakneck speed and luckily were not caught.

That year, my friends Ray Campbell and Forrest Watson talked me into asking Marlys Peterson to the prom. Because I couldn't dance, their dates, Cathy Moen and Bev Carlson, gave me a kindergarten-level crash course on rudimentary dancing. Wearing a suit and tie and armed with minimum dancing skill and a car (the Champ), I picked up Marlys at her home on Central Avenue. She was perfectly beautiful. It was not in the power of Nature to give any addition to her charms and I was speechless. We were both excited, nervous and unsure of ourselves. Her folks were not home. As she closed the door, she moved forward, but suddenly stopped.

The devil must have been lurking near, for his evening dose of humor. When she closed the door, her formal got caught in it! It was probably the best-fitting front door in Red Wing. I pulled on her formal. I tried raising the door. I tried to pry the door up. I checked the back door and all the windows but to no avail. It was time for us to be at Ray's for predance snack. Marlys said, "Tear it." The rip took a good chunk out of the bottom. It created a lot of conversation that night. "Little early, wasn't it, Milt?" I was gaining a reputation as *The Playboy of the Western World*.

Our first dance went reasonably well, considering the earlier event. My minimal social graces extended to asking Bev and Cathy to dance, as my instructors wanted to see if I had retained any of their training.

I never followed up with Marlys. She was pretty, smart and active in school affairs. Perhaps it was too many stressful memories on the dance floor. Shuffle and turn! Shuffle and turn! The next year I asked a girl—who remains nameless in my memory—to our Senior Prom, but someone beat me to the tender morsel and I never got around to asking anyone else.

In high school, farm kids were under a real handicap. City classmates had years of early sports and musical training that we were never exposed to. As a result, we were so far behind we never tried out for sports. I usually took five courses, although only four were required.

Bob and Barbara. "We were always concerned that a phone call might come from the War Department, with Bob in the military. We'd be relieved when we got a letter from him. It was postmarked in either New York or San Francisco, so we only knew that he was somewhere in the Atlantic or Pacific."

One year I took six. I never was an A student but usually make the B honor roll. I got Cs in Math, As in history, biology and chemistry. My best report card was 2 As, 2 Bs, and 1 C.

I enjoyed journalism and wrote a humor column with Dibba Erickson called Milt and Dibba's Corner; that gave me a little fame. Dibba and I went back and reworked jokes from old Chieftans. We rebuilt them, using current names and events with some of our own originals.

In 10th grade, Naomi Carlson sat behind me in history, which was not her forte. She was prepared for a D. I'd change her answers or she'd leave most everything blank and I filled in the correct ones. She rarely had to change any for me to get my A.

Milt and Wilbur.

I enjoyed typing, because I'd watch the teacher's backside wiggle every time she walked up to the front of the room. She was young, nice-looking and had a somewhat sinful expression. It was even more stimulating watching her butt gyrate after we heard she had been bedding down with a sailor who was home on leave.

In the night, all cats are gray!

> In ecstasy he caught her in his arms.
> His heart went bathing in a bath of blisses
> And melted in a hundred thousand kisses.
> And she responded in the fullest measure
> With all that could delight or give him pleasure.
> - *Canterbury Tales*

Miss Stroble, who let Naomi and me exchange history test papers was a foxy lady and I liked her. That's probably why I did well in her class. "How the beauty that your clothes conceal is like a spark that sets afire my heart" Rabelais. Another beauty was a first-year teacher Sylvia Vathing, who was a vision of delight, both day and night. The other teachers ignored her because she made the rest look so plain and old, like walking corpses!

I lost at least one grade point from my teacher Signe Anderson, when I was in 12th grade English. I did a book report on Marie Antoinette. I stood in front of the class telling of a courtesan's love life who liked sex 18 times a day! By the time I got into a discussion of the pros and cons and whether this was even possible, the class was in an uproar and she stopped me. Hell, it was my day in the sun.

During my junior or senior year, older girls would smile and wave at me as I drove around town in the Champion. It must have been Willy who was *The Playboy of the Western World*, and we didn't even know it! We had gas rationing during the war and illegally put tractor gas in the Champion. After we were out, Dad always checked the mileage. I'd usually asked to go to a movie in Red Wing, which was 14 miles, and then drive out to The Trianon or over to the Valencia Ballroom. I'd drive 16 miles and stop and disconnect the odometer. One night I forgot to reconnect it. Dad took it into the garage, found out that it had been disconnected and I lost car privileges for a long time. After that, I had to rely on Merlin and his dad's '36 Ford.

For us, the war was not too much of a hardship. We had the new Champion and we traded butter and meat with Red Wing people for ration coupons that we used to buy gas and sugar.

We were always concerned that a phone call might come from the War Department, with Bob in the military. We'd be relieved when we got a letter from him. It was postmarked in either New York or San Francisco, so we only knew that he was somewhere in the Atlantic or Pacific. From time to time, Bob would send me $2 to $10 while I was in high school. He said he remembered what a bitch it was to have no money.

I have three regrets about things I missed in high school. I never learned to play a musical instrument. I never tried out for a class play (two every year). My biggest mistake was I should have taken Latin. Later, a U of M instructor told me, "Latin is the foundation of the English language."

Willy and Edith were hard-working A students. Bob's only A came from Harry Howe's wood shop. Adeline got good grades, but I think she always got an extra grade from "brown-nosing" teachers like Richard Lundquist and Groettum. The older teachers remembered earlier Haymans and first gave me an automatic A then rapidly learned I belonged in the B column.

During my senior year on V-J Day (Victory over Japan Day), Willy took me to Red Wing's celebrations. Fran had learned there was a party at Dr. Dart's cabin down on Lake Pepin.

> "And in thy shady cell, where none can spy him,
> Sits sin, to seize the soul that wanders by him." Samuel Butler

There sin was masquerading under the guise of LuAnn Dart. If God ever made a woman for the sole art of pleasure, she filled this most wondrous design. Most of the couples were attached. LuAnn saw me standing there in all my virginal purity and analyzed the situation with clarion speed. I might be a throw-away toy to celebrate V-J night. She lured me into a bedroom and locked the door. Things went from good to gooder and I soon realized she would not take "No" for an answer.

All the horrors Bob and Willy told me about girls ran through my mind: pregnancy, disease, shotgun wedding, sin and headlines in the *Eagle*, "Farm Boy Rapes Doctor's Daughter in Lakeside Bordello." Although the anodyne, in the form of LuAnn, was fast working astride my sinless body, the greatest fear now entered my heated brain. What if LuAnn might be equipped with the "vagina dentata" of misogynistic legend.

Milt in the Army 1946 to 1948. "Two years in the Army were followed by a college education at the University of Minnesota."

Then, someone knocked on the door to report a telephone call. This act saved my virginity, but only by a nat's hair! Willy and Fran's car was water-logged and had a wet carburetor near Frontenac and Tom Comstock would pick me up shortly!

Two years in the Army were followed by a college education at the University of Minnesota.

My junior year, I was out with the boys on Friday evening. We were at a small bar called the Hoop-de-doo which had a small dance floor and a jukebox. There was a table full of girls in the dark room. Then I saw her through the mist and smoke and said, or rather Homer said,

"My junior year in college, I was out with the boys when I saw her through the mist and smoke. We danced. We laughed and smiled. We glowed. We embraced our bodies tightly on the dance floor and at the end of the evening, taking her home, I said to myself, she was a goddess without their twisted wiles."

"Oh Apollo, if only!" the giant killer cried.
"Archer, bind me down with triple these endless chains! Let all you gods look on, and all you goddesses too. How I'd love to bed that Golden Aphrodite!"

We danced. We laughed and smiled. We glowed. We embraced our bodies tightly on the dance floor and at the end of the evening, taking her home, I said to myself, she was a goddess without their twisted wiles. And as Cervantes said,

"This was good luck knocking at the door and I was going to let it in."

We had beautiful moonlight nights at Lake Nokomis. One of the highlights of our courtship was the ROTC ball at the Radisson:

> She was anointed with oil.
> Ambrosial oil, the bloom that clings
> To the gods who never die
> And swathed round in a gown to stop the heart
> An ecstasy—a vision. Homer

As everyone knows, the road to "Will you have each other until death…" has some hills and valleys. Contrary to the Bible, the path is not straight, but has curves. And as to whether the Gate is wide or narrow, I couldn't say and now could care less.

And many years later—more of Homer:

> "If it's bed you want," reserved Penelope replied,
> "It's bed you'll have, when the spirit moves"
>   —Rejoicing in each other, they returned to their bed
> The old familiar place they loved so well.

No Place — Saving the Best Fort to Last!
By son Tom Hayman

Dad and Bob came up with the idea of building a warming shack on the ski trails, and it grew over the years and evolved into a popular neighborhood meeting place. "No Place" was coined when Bill Steele, a Maiden Rock neighbor, and Dad would stay out late "socializing" and the wives would ask where they had been, to which they replied,
"No Place"—hence the name.

No Place.

Much like forts they'd built in years past, "No Place" was built from re-used, recycled and reclaimed materials sourced from wherever they could find them. The metal siding was from old farm buildings. Windows were rejects or seconds picked up at a local lumber company. "No Place" featured an eclectic collection of wall posters from world travel destinations, operas, beautiful women, and more. The place was stocked with snacks, food and liquor and became a great spot to warm ourselves when skiing or hiking or simply relaxing with a libation.

No Place Interior.

Word about the shack got out and the neighbors started to join in. It brought the whole neighborhood together, eventually requiring an addition to accommodate everyone. It was a great place to regale friends with old stories and to make new ones! It was also popular with mice and bats which added to the ambiance of the place. It was Dad's and Bob's last fling with their boyhood building skills and became a real social spot on the hill! They indeed saved their best fort to last!

Maiden Rock Neighbors

Sid and Grace, our old neighbors in Maiden Rock, always had interesting stories. There was one about two old bachelors with a collie that was old. Neither one wanted to shoot their old friend, so they took her out in a field, tied a stick of dynamite onto her tail and lit the fuse. The sound of the burning fuse scared her and she took off for home, crawled under the porch and blew the porch off the house!

Sid had worked in the Southwest, driving from one town to another and he'd see this sweet old Mexican lady with a big basket of eggs. It became his habit to pick her up and take her to town every week, for which she was very appreciative. Later, he learned she had jars of homemade tequila under the eggs and was bootlegging in the next town.

Grace grew up near the Maiden Rock property and told about the fun they had sledding behind our farm. Six neighbors would get together and pull an old horse cutter to the top of a ridge, then ride it down to the bottom of the hill. They'd do it again, over and over. Occasionally it tipped over and they'd right it and go again.

One night they slipped over to the bluff to Jim Haugen's place and tied 17 sticks of dynamite in one tree and 18 sticks in another. They lit both fuses, expecting them to go off all at once, but instead there were two big explosions, which woke up all of Maiden Rock, or it might better be said, blew them out of bed!

Bob gave Sid a picture of a nude blonde. Sid named her "Ethel" and hung her in the south sewing room. Sitting in the kitchen, Sid would ask King, their dog, "Where's Ethel?" King would walk into the other room, sit on his butt and look up at Ethel. Sid had a falling out with Jim when he called him a no-account, worthless so-and-so. Sid threw a double shot of brandy in his face. Country living can get pretty exciting!

Sid had an old dog called Tip and he'd tell him to go out on the ice to test it. Tip would walk out and jump with all four legs bouncing up and down simultaneously. Sid also made friends with a ruffed grouse

Milt and Marilyn's Holiday Card from 1977 shows Milt's humor in attempting to replicate "The American Gothic" by Norman Rockwell.

that lived near our barn. He'd rattle the tailgate of his pickup and the grouse would come out of the woods, hop up on the tailgate and then onto Sid's shoulder and peck his ear. One day Grace rattled the tailgate, the grouse came out, saw her, turned around and went back into the woods.

Sid and Grace always welcomed visitors with a cup of coffee and some sweets. Once Grace was alone, the neighbors still visited. Monday mornings became a regular time to meet, gossip and exchange stories. The people on the hill continue the tradition, meeting every other Monday at alternating homes.

One morning, in March of 2001, someone mentioned a 90-year old acquaintance who had just gone to Ellsworth to take her driver's test to renew her license. They caught her cheating! Her car was all beat up from so many fender benders. She still goes to the rest homes and brings food and presents to the lockups! Then, there's another character who goes to all the funerals to eat, then stuffs food in her big purse and steals toilet paper from the church lavatory!

For critics who may say my story contains too much sex, I end with this: "It's Love and Love alone that makes the world go round." Steven Foster

Milt, Marilyn and Bob. Happy summer days.

La commedia è finita!
The comedy is finished!

"30"
Journalists used "30" to mean "end" or "no more;" it originated in Western Union's "92 Code" of 1859.

Christmas Pudding

Every year since the 1860s, an English Christmas pudding has been made without fail by the Haymans. It was so important it was even made during the Depression. It was always Gim's job. The day before Christmas she cut all the fruit up. Then very early Christmas morning, she got up, lit the wood stove and put the canner on. The water had to be boiling by 4 o' clock because the pudding had to boil for 7 to 8 hours. We usually ate at 12 o' clock and it had to be done by then.

Nowadays, we make it a week ahead and warm it up for our Christmas. Gim never had a failure. It was always excellent.

When it was done, we'd have a great big kettle of snow water and the pudding was plunged into this a couple of times to set it and cool the outside. We put it on a plate, pulled off the towel and you hopefully had a beautiful plum pudding!

The sauce we liked best was made from raspberry juice and thickened with either flour or cornstarch. Some butter, salt, sugar and brandy was added at the end. Some years when there was no raspberry crop we had to use a bottle of wine, but we never liked that as well.

Without fail, "every year since the 1860s, an English Christmas pudding has been made by the Haymans. It was so important it was made during the Depression." In the early years, it was Gim's job who passed it to Dora, then Marilyn. Tom and Martha now maintain this family tradition.

Marilyn's Christmas Pudding Recipe with Instructions

Ingredients

2 ½ cups ground shaved suet

5 cups flour

2 ½ cups sugar

2 cups chopped dates, currants and citron

2 cups (found at Barlow's Rochester) seedless raisins Seeded Muscat raisins from Sun Maid

1 ½ teaspoons salt

1 ½ teaspoons allspice

1 ½ teaspoons cinnamon

½ teaspoon cloves

1 teaspoon nutmeg

2 teaspoons baking powder

2 tablespoons molasses

4 eggs

Enough milk 1 cup to make a batter. Collect in bottom of dish.

Fill a canner ¾ full of water. Bring to a boil. Have trivet in the canner to keep the pudding off bottom.

In a 10-qt bowl, mix together the fruit, suet, sugar and spices. Then add and mix flour. Beat 4 eggs, add molasses and slowly add a cup of hot milk. Slowly mix eggs and milk into the dry ingredients. Looks like a fruit cake.

Muslin-like cloth @ 2.5 sq ft. (Gim used a cloth made from a heavy sugar sack.) Rinse in cold water. Dust with flour. Drape over a large bowl—at least five quarts. Pour mixture onto the cloth. Pull together corners. Tie off with about 1 inch of space between batter and tie point. Slowly immerse into boiling water.

First hour turn every 15 minutes. Then turn every half hour for six hours. Remove and put into a snow filled container and let sit for two minutes. Cut string and carefully pull away cloth. Invert onto a plate. Don't cover—let it cool.

The desired pudding is about the size of a volleyball. Cut in half, then in pieces. Cover with syrup. Can be reheated in an oven, covered, with a little water in the corner.

Syrup

Heat one quart raspberry juice with butter and sugar. Thicken with cornstarch. Add ½ to 1 cup brandy. Should be like syrup.

Epilogue

Milt wasn't in tune with churches and dogma but did believe in a Creator. You can call it God. He had a great respect and awe for all creation, especially in the wooded hills where he communed with his God like his father, Charles, who said his heart and soul could be found in the sand hill. He admired the great red oaks, symbols of strength and beauty that grew there. Now he rests under a red oak. We will never forget him. We will always love him. Each, in your own way, please pray for his eternal peace. May you find a better understanding of this complicated man through the stories he shared in this book.

So what happened to Milt and his siblings later in life? Immediately follows a brief synopsis of their lives.

We hope you enjoyed reading this book.

With thanks and gratitude,
Marilyn Hayman and son, Tom Hayman

One of my reasons for writing this book was "this was a time, that ever was or ever will be, of the greatest changes in farming history. We went from oxen and horses-used for thousands of years-to jet travel and placing a man on the moon. All in one generation."

"Some people call those the good ole' days. If they call those days good, they have forgotten the hardship. If they call those days good they remember the tight family bonds that living and working close together forged."

So what became of the people in this book?

Bob, Adeline, Milt, Janet and Wilbur.

Milton John Hayman

Born: May 17, 1928 Died: March 26, 2012
Married: Marilyn Jeanne Fiedler, October 25, 1952
Family: Thomas Jon Hayman, born August 11, 1953

Milt went into the Army right out of high school for two years and then the University of Minnesota; then worked in lumber sales in Minneapolis.

Marilyn got a B.A. in Education from Downer College in Milwaukee in 1950 and a Masters in Educational Psychology in 1977. She taught in elementary schools in Minneapolis for twenty years and then in Special Education for another 10.

They lived in Richfield, built a house in Prior Lake and retired to Maiden Rock, WI, where subsequently brother Bob and wife Barbara, later settled.

Robert William Hayman

Born: March 25, 1918 Died: December 11, 2003
Married: Barbara Ann Cobb, July 3, 1946
Family: Robert William Hayman Jr. (Bill), born June 29, 1951
         Jonathan Cobb Hayman, born April 8, 1953

Bob was a navy pilot during WWII. During the war he served as a carrier pilot. He received honors for sinking a Nazi sub in the Atlantic off the Azores. He flew for Pan Am while living on Long Island, NY, and then retired to Maiden Rock, WI, building a home next to Milt and Marilyn.

Barbara was a homemaker and was active as a volunteer with various charities.

Wilbur Henry Hayman

Born: January 31, 1920 Died: November 30, 2007
Married: Francis Johnson, October 20, 1945
Family: Daniel Hayman, born October 8, 1949
   Jean Elizabeth Hayman, born October 25, 1952

Wilbur took over the family farm from Charles and Dora. He is best remembered sitting on a cold fall day, harvesting corn with a two-row Unisheller corn picker wearing a heavy jean jacket and stocking cap knitted by Franny. The farm was sold to nephew Niles Deden and Wilbur and Franny retired into Red Wing, MN.

Franny graduated from the St John's Hospital School of Nursing in 1944 as an R.N. She worked at the Interstate Medical Center in Red Wing for 28 years.

Edith Marie Hayman

Born: February 24, 1922 Died: January 10, 1944

Edith graduated from high school at age 16. After one year of Teacher Training she began teaching at School District 113 along Hay Creek at the age of 17, where she was younger than her oldest students! She loved to write to foreign pen pals and was an intelligent woman who died too young.

Adeline Dorothea Sophia Hayman Deden

Born: March 19, 1924 Died: March 21, 2016
Married: Vincent Edward Deden, August 14, 1946
Family: Niles Vincent Deden, born April 25, 1949
   Jerome Charles Deden, born January 3, 1952
   Ross Edward Deden, born February 15, 1954

Adeline taught school in a one-room school house, was a homemaker and was active with the Goodhue County Historical Society. She is best remembered for her joy in sharing meals with family and friends. She believed in the importance of family get-togethers and maintaining family ties.

Vince operated the Deden farm. He and Adeline both managed the Hay Creek Mutual Insurance Company for 22 years. They retired to a home built on the farm by Niles and Sue, who moved into the original farm house and took over the farm.

Janet May Hayman Golisch

Born: July 10, 1938 Died: April 16, 1999
Married: David Richard Golisch, June 30, 1962
Family: Lisa Ann Golisch Trueblood, born May 29, 1963
   Sara May Ester Golisch Heintz, born February 4, 1964
   Timothy David Golisch, born July 18, 1968
   Benjamin Richard Golisch, born September 21, 1970

Janet graduated from Bethany College, Mankato, MN, and taught school for four years. She was a homemaker, worked at a farm market and at Kohls. She was an encourager and had a love of stories and music.

David graduated from Bethany College, Mankato, MN, and from Valparaiso University with a degree in Education in 1961. He taught math and science for fifteen years before becoming a computer programmer and systems analyst for companies in Michigan and Wisconsin.

Glossary

All eras of history have their own terms and words that are unique to them. This glossary is meant as a resource to guide you through the unfamiliar words and phrases of this time. It is our hope that this additional information will make these stories all the more interesting to you. *Definitions gleaned from FarmCollector.com, Google searches and interviews with farmers.*

Glossary Word *(found on page #)*	**Definition**
Al Capp *(p.68)*	An American cartoonist and humorist whose comic strip "Li'l Abner" ran in newspapers from 1934 to 1977.
anvil and forge *(p.30)*	An anvil is a large block of iron or steel with a flat top used to shape metal by placing the metal piece on it and striking it with a hammer. A forge uses flames to shape metal.
augered *(p.22, 35)*	An auger is a tool consisting of a twisted, spiral rod of metal attached to a handle, used on farms for carrying grain from wagons to a bin or granary.
band saw *(p.30)*	Consists of an endless toothed steel band passing over two wheels used to cut wood or metal and also to cut and trim meat.
Basswood *(p.53)*	A North American linden tree whose wood can be easily shaped.
binder *(p.21, 24, 29, 33, 34, 35)*	A machine used to cut grain and bind it into bundles.
Birch *(p. 45, 48, 53, 58)*	A thin-leaved hardwood tree used for lumber, veneer and plywood.
blower pipe *(p. 34)*	A tube through which forced air was used to move fodder.
bow saw *(p. 32)*	A narrow saw stretched like a bowstring on a light frame, especially good for cutting tree branches.
burr mill *(p. 9)*	A type of grinder that uses two abrasive surfaces, or burrs, to grind hard, small food items.
castrated *(p.11)*	A castrated bull is a steer whose testicles have been removed, making it unable to reproduce. Castrating boar pigs takes a sharp taste out of the meat and lessens aggression.
chaff *(p. 18, 22, 23, 59)*	The seed coverings and other debris separated from the seed itself when threshing grain.
cistern *(p. 4, 10, 27, 31, 45, 55, 57)*	An underground water storage tank used to store rainwater (soft water) for household use.
Civilian Conservation Corps (CCC) *(p. 39, 67)*	Part of FDR's New Deal Program, the CCC allowed single men between the ages of 18 and 25 to enlist in work programs to improve America's public lands, forests and parks.
corn beef *(p. 73)*	Beef brisket that's been cured in a salt brine with spices to tenderize and add flavor.
corn binder *(p. 33)*	A farm implement used to harvest corn. It has a cutter and a device for packing and tying the stalks into bundles.

Glossary

Glossary Word *(found on page #)*	Definition
corn shredder *(p. 30, 34)*	A farm implement that cuts the corn stalks to use as food for cattle.
cotter pins *(p. 49)*	Split metal pins that are opened out after being passed through a hole. The pins fasten two things together.
cottonwood vs oak	Cottonwoods are poplars whose root system is shallow, soft and unstable during storms and prone to rot. Its wood is lightweight, soft and prone to warping. Oak trees have strong root systems. Oak wood is strong, hard and heavy with a dense grain, resistant to insects and shrinkage.
cream *(p. 10, 35, 80, 83)*	After milking, cow's milk would settle over time so the cream rose to the top. This cream was used to make butter.
crowbars *(p. 29, 31)*	An iron bar with a flattened end used as a lever.
curing/cured (meats) *(p. 2, 3, 24, 52)*	Meat was hung in the small shed or smokehouse and a low smoky fire was kept burning for several weeks.
curry *(p. 27)*	To curry a horse is to clean its coat with a special comb with many small teeth.
dehorned *(p. 11)*	Dehorning is done to young calves to prevent injuries to other cattle as well as the person tending to the cattle.
dime store *(p. 41)*	Dime stores such as Woolworth's sold inexpensive goods; often, the highest price was a dime.
dragged the fields *(p. 13)*	A drag is a farm implement that uses many flexible iron teeth to smooth the ground as well as loosen it after it's been plowed and packed.
draw shave *(p. 27, 48)*	A draw shave has two handles which are drawn up toward the user. The angle used controls the depth of cut.
dry well *(p. 1)*	A large hole on the ground, usually lined on the sides with concrete or brick. An underground pipe carries water to the dry well, where it can be turned on or off.
dump bucket *(p. 25)*	An attachment that scoops grain and releases it into a chosen area.
feed mill *(p. 9, 30, 35)*	A feed mill grinds feed for livestock on the farm.
field pitcher *(p. 21)*	A field pitcher pitches hay or sheaves onto a cart or a wagon.
flax *(p. 23)*	A flowering plant which may be used to make rope, twine, linen or even bank notes.
fodder *(p. 21, 29, 34, 46)*	A type of food for livestock such as straw, hay, grass or silage made from farming or agricultural processes.

Glossary

Glossary Word (found on page #)	Definition
Gold Stars *(p. 39)*	Mothers (including stepmothers, foster mothers, or adoptive mothers) whose children died while serving in action are known as Gold Star mothers.
granary *(p. 3, 9, 14, 22, 23, 24, 27)*	A granary is a farm building used solely for storing threshed grain such as oats or wheat.
hay fork *(p. 18)*	A metal clamp used to pull large volumes of hay off a wagon and move it into the barn, using ropes and pulleys. (See set fork).
hay rake *(p. 14, 18, 19, 30, 32, 51)* *aka rake, dump rake or side delivery rake*	A tool hooked to a tractor which rakes cut hay into windrows and can turn the hay so it dries. A side delivery rakes is a rake with teeth on a reel. The teeth lift and push the hay to the side into a windrow at right angles to the forward path of the rake.
hay vs. straw	Hay is composed of dried grasses such as timothy or alfalfa; straw is composed of dried grain stalks of oats or wheat.
hell and brimstone *(p. 36, 43)*	This refers to Christian preaching that warns of damnation to hell and its torture and suffering. The intent is to make listeners eager to repent. Brimstone means "burning stone".
hog scraper *(p. 1, 62)*	A tool used to remove the small hairs from a pig's carcass after slaughter.
horse and stone boat *(p. 17, 33)*	A stone boat is a flat sled or sledge pulled by horses used to haul heavy loads over hard or soft ground or snow.
humus *(p. 26)*	A dark, organic substance that occurs when plant and animal matter decays. It improves soil health and fertility and helps soil retain air and water.
husking bee *(p. 34)*	A gathering of farm families or friends to husk corn.
indentured *(p. 44)*	A form of labor in which the worker is contracted to work without pay for a number of years.
iron "S" *(p. 1)*	An S hook is used to hang items on a pole such as kettles on an open fire.
June grass *(p. 18)*	A native prairie grass with silvery green seed heads.
lathe *(p. 30)*	A lathe is a machine tool that rotates a piece around an axis to shape it with a stationary cutting tool.
linen chest *(p. 13)*	A place to store any linens such as sheets or pillow cases.
lodge *(p. 24)*	"The rye didn't lodge much." Lodging occurs when grain's root systems fail or the stalks buckle, causing the grain to bend or lie flat, making harvest difficult and causing loss of yield.

Glossary

Glossary Word *(found on page #)*	Definition
loft *(p. 9, 19, 29)*	*Calf barn loft.* A small space above the main floor of a barn, stable or shed, used to store hay, straw or other fodder for animals.
loggia *(p. 15)*	A covered outdoor space that may be attached to a building or stand alone.
lugs *(p. 23, 34)*	*Steel lugs.* Individual thick pieces of steel placed on a tractor's large wheels acted as cleats, allowing the tractor to gain traction and pulling power through a field.
manure spreader *(p. 10, 35)*	A piece of machinery that distributes manure across fields as fertilizer.
maul *(p. 5, 29)*	A heavy hammer with one wedge-shaped end used to split wood.
meat saw *(p. 1)*	Also called a butcher's saw or a bone saw, a saw used to cut through meat and bone when butchering on the farm.
milk dishes *(p. 80)*	Prior to automation, every part of milking a dairy herd was done by hand; each piece of equipment had to be washed thoroughly, including the cups placed on the cow's teats to draw out the milk; the hoses that brought the milk to pails; the separators that held discs that separated the milk from the cream; and any containers that would hold the milk, such as shotgun cans. Anything that needed to be washed might be considered milk dishes, as opposed to kitchen dishes.
Minnesota hay loader *(p. 19)*	A farm implement for gathering hay from a windrow or swath and loading it onto a wagon.
mothballs *(p. 13)*	Small pellets, often made of naphthalene, used to keep away moths. The pellets smell like bug repellent.
octagon wire *(p. 58)*	A type of barb wire which has eight sides rather than a round shape.
outhouse *(p. 32, 46, 65, 71)*	An outdoor building that housed a toilet, with no plumbing.
overburden *(p. 29)*	*"First we removed the overburden."* The layer of rock, soil or grasses that lie above the limestone.
party line *(p. 81, 82)*	A telephone line shared by 2 or more parties. Each household had a unique ring.
pepper and yellow peppercorns *(p. 1, 3)*	Dried berries of a climbing vine used as preservatives for centuries because of their antimicrobial and antioxidant properties.
prison twine *(p. 33)* *Also binder twine (p. 4) and twine (p. 20, 21, 34, 48)*	In Minnesota, binder twine was made by prisoners at Stillwater State Prison. In 1937, approximately 600 prisoners made approximately 25,000,000 pounds of twine.
pulley *(p. 1, 5, 18, 19, 21, 22, 30)*	A wheel that carries a flexible rope, cord, cable, chain or belt on its rim.

Glossary

Glossary Word *(found on page #)*	Definition
punks *(p. 7)*	Smoldering sticks used to light fuses, much safer than a match because of their length.
quack grass *(p. 27)*	A creeping perennial grass, considered an aggressive weed which spreads vigorously through underground rhizomes.
Red Owl bread *(p. 49)*	Red Owl was a grocery store, headquartered in Hopkins, Minnesota, open from the 1920s through the 1980s.
roller head *(p. 34)*	Attached to the corn shredder, the roller head pulled the corn along its way through the machine.
rope fork *(p. 18)*	A pulley system held a rope attached in the hay mow to a horse on the ground at the back of the barn. The rope was attached to a fork (see set fork). The signal was given for the horse to pull, which sent the hay into the mow to be released.
rye *(p. 9, 21, 22, 24)*	A cereal plant that tolerates poor soil and low temperatures.
saw horses *(p. 1, 32)*	Sturdy frames used to support boards
set fork *(p. 18)*	The end of the pulley system in a hay mow which would be tamped into the bales or loose hay to hold the hay as it was lifted into the barn by rope on the pulleys.
shocking of grain *(p. 4)*	When farmers manually cut sheaves of grain, the sheaves were tied into bundles and stacked against one another vertically to create a "shock" so the sheaves could air dry to be preserved.
shredder *(p. 35)*	A motorized mechanical tool that cuts, rolls, tears and ejects unwanted vegetation.
silt *(p. 48)*	A solid, dust-like sediment that water, ice and wind transport and deposit.
slash *(p. 7)*	*Logs and slash.* Brush and other vegetation. Non-usable tree parts; branches.
sloe-eyed *(p. 37)*	Sloe-eyed is blue-eyed.
smokehouse *(p. 2, 10, 57)*	A small building on a farm used to smoke, salt and store meat and fish.
snapping rollers *(p. 34)*	Harvest tools used to separate the ear of corn from the stalk.
soft water *(p. 31)*	Cisterns caught rainwater, which had fewer minerals than groundwater. The soft water helped soap to lather to wash clothes, dishes or people.
spring toothings *(p. 27)*	Spring toothings are mounted in rows on a harrow and used to break up the soil for planting.
square *(p. 29)*	*(for building)* A square has an L-shape that allows carpenters to create angles when building.

Glossary

Glossary Word *(found on page #)*	**Definition**
stock dip *(p. 11, 31)*	A liquid used to prevent infection.
stone hammer *(p. 29)*	A large hammer, possibly with one tapered side, to cut stone into smaller chunks or squares.
stonemason *(p. 1)*	An individual who builds structures out of stone.
stucco *(p. 30)*	A fine plaster used for coating walls.
sulky plow *(p. 13, 27)*	A steel, horse-drawn plow with two wheels and a seat for the driver.
Swede saw *(p. 32)*	A type of bow saw, a crosscut saw with a metal frame and a wide, coarse blade shaped like a bow, also known as a bucksaw or Finn saw.
tedder *(p. 18, 30)*	A machine that lifts and spreads hay to enable it to dry better.
thresher's shaft boxes *(p. 25)*	The thresher's shaft and gears were covered by a metal box. These moving parts had to be lubricated to prevent overheating.
threshing *(p. 19, 21, 22, 23, 24, 25, 26, 27, 28)*	Separating grain such as wheat or oats from the plant.
torque *(p. 6)*	*(torque against the blade)* A measure of the force that can cause an object to rotate on an axis. The amount of pressure used on the log when feeding the buzz saw needed to be constant and precise to prevent accidents.
vise *(p. 30, 31)*	A tool with movable jaws which can be tightened to hold an object while work is done on it.
wedges and a splitting maul *(p. 5)* *Also wedges (p. 23, 29) and maul (p. 5, 29, 99)*	A wedge is a tool with a flat, often square, top that tapers to a narrow, ax-like end. The narrow end is placed on a chunk of log and the top is hit with a large hammer, splitting the log. A splitting maul looks like a combination sledgehammer and wedge and is used to split logs.
winter wheat *(p. 21)*	Winter wheat is planted in the fall, lives through winter and is harvested in spring.
winterized the stock tank *(p. 35)*	All livestock needs water, even in winter. To keep the water from freezing, farmers would cover the tank at night with horse blankets, buffalo hides or whatever they had at hand.
witchgrass *(p. 18, 27)*	A tough, creeping grass that can become an invasive weed.
Works Progress Administration (WPA) *(p. 39, 67)*	The Works Progress Administration was a New Deal Program created by FDR to help the unemployed during the Depression.

www.ingramcontent.com/pod-product-compliance
Lightning Source LLC
Chambersburg PA
CBRC100812010526
44107CB00023B/1269